EXPLORING BUDDHISM

The Buddhist field of knowledge is now so vast that few can master all of it, and the study and application of its principles must be a matter of choice.

One may choose the magnificent moral philosophy of Theravada. the oldest school, or the Zen training of Japan; or special themes such as the doctrine of No-self, the Mahayana emphasis on compassion or the universal law of Karma and Rebirth. But the intense self-discipline needed for true spiritual experience calls for specialisation of subject and technique.

In his latest work Christmas Humphreys, the well-known author of a dozen books on Buddhism (including such popular volumes as *Buddhism, The Buddhist Way of Life, Zen Buddhism* and *A Western Approach to Zen*) describes his exploration in some 20 of these subjects, which together form a valuable addition to Western Buddhist literature. Some of these chapters deal with ideas not hitherto expressed—but, as the author points out, all experience is purely personal and therefore fresh to the reader's mind.

This is a book for all in the West who are finding in Buddhism a tested system of truth which accords with the highest discoveries of science and psychology and also with the deepest nature of man.

Exploring Buddhism

CHRISTMAS HUMPHREYS

A QUEST BOOK

Published under a grant from the Kern Foundation

THE THEOSOPHICAL PUBLISHING HOUSE
Wheaton, Ill., U.S.A.
Madras, India / London, England

© Christmas Humphreys 1974

First Quest Edition published by the Theosophical Publishing House, Wheaton, Illinois, a department of The Theosophical Society in America, 1974.

Humphreys, Christmas, 1901-
Exploring Buddhism.

(A Quest book)
1. Buddha and Buddhism.   I. Title.
BQ4022.H85 1975   294.3   74-12206
ISBN 0-8356-0454-3

PRINTED IN THE UNITED STATES OF AMERICA

Contents

Acknowledgements

I am deeply grateful to those who have fair-copied my original typing, often with helpful criticism. In particular I would mention Miss Pat Wilkinson, Mrs Millicent Hamilton-Bradbury and Mrs Muriel Clark. I am equally grateful to Mr George Porte for photographing material to save typing.

I must also thank the Editors of the periodicals in which certain of these chapters first appeared. They include the *American Theosophist*, *The Ceylon Wesak Annual*, the *Journal of the Maha Bodhi Society*, *The Middle Way* and *The Theosophist*.

Introduction

In the course of centuries the Buddhist field has become so vast that it is difficult to write about *all* of it. Few indeed have attempted to do so, and the number of books which even include all its schools and wanderings is remarkably small. By now the word Buddhist has come to bear two very different meanings: (1) Buddhist scholars, learned men and women who choose some corner of the field and add to our knowledge of it. They are trained to write objectively, and few would even admit to being Buddhists in the second meaning of the term. (2) This includes students who attempt to obtain confirmation of doctrine by diving into their own minds and by applying the principles examined in their own lives. For want of a better term one may call them practitioners. But no one attempting to practise Buddhism can operate in the entire field. There must be, as with scholars, specialization, concentration on a chosen area. One may, for example, practise the basic teachings of the Theravada, which is the Buddhism of Ceylon, Burma and Thailand, and generally accepted as the oldest Buddhist school extant; or one may attempt the Zen training open to Westerners in Japan; or one may try the still harder practice of Tibetan Buddhism, but one cannot seriously practise all three at once. The intensive self-discipline needed for acquiring real spiritual experience calls for specialization before theory can be developed into actual awareness. Whether the specialized target be a theme, such as No-self or the Void, or Karma and Rebirth, or as wide as a school with its own special 'way', the studies must be in depth.

For myself, in half a century of exploration in the spiritual continent of Buddhism I have, conditioned by my own past lives and self-training in this one, made intensive expeditions into the theory and the practice of selected corners of the field. Herein are accounts of such explorings. This is not, therefore, another textbook of Buddhism, and large areas of that field are scarcely mentioned. In the subjects chosen there are, of course, repetitions, for the same features, as of landscape, appear again and again. And in describing these adventures my own equipment—one might almost call it an intellectual pharmacopoeia—of quotations and the like may well be repeated.

Per contra, there may be seeming contradictions, for there are, as scholars and practitioners alike will agree, considerable areas of Buddhism where conflicting views are strongly held, and in the tolerant atmosphere of Buddhism frankly compared and discussed. For example, the Anatta doctrine of the Theravada school as still taught in parts of it today is, some hold, the heart of Buddhism or, as others argue, demonstrably untrue. Again, the Tantras of Tibet are basic Tibetan Buddhism or a totally unBuddhist importation from India. Or Shin Buddhism, most popular in Japan, is either a legitimate complement to Zen Buddhism, or so widely at variance with the spirit of Buddhism as a whole that it should be excluded from the ambit of that term. So views can differ widely on the legitimate purpose and value of meditation, on the need for a branch of the Theravada Sangha in the West, or on the relation of Buddhist philosophy to modern physics.

What, then, in this work is original? In one sense nothing and in another sense all. Doctrine may be flogged to a standstill, but all experience is entirely personal, and fresh for the individual each time that timeless moment arrives. Buddhism knows no authority save that of the intuition and every step on the Way must be trodden by the seeker until intensive personal knowledge ratifies its truth.

My explorations have at times been in areas trodden flat,

one might say, by two thousand years of experience and description, yet always the approach is new. These might include the chapters on Anatta, Karma and Rebirth, and Concentration and Meditation. Yet no two explorers approach their subject in quite the same way, nor achieve precisely the same understanding.

In other subjects, such as that of the 'Wisdom that has gone Beyond', the field is less well trodden, and it is all too easy to lose one's way, while if the two concentric circles of Tibetan Buddhism as described in Chapter 3 have been so described elsewhere I have never read such a description.

Here then is food for different types and states of mind, some items rescued from the silence of back volumes of magazines, some built up from unfinished articles, some new. May some of them at least be of service to all who seek the Beyond of gross materialism, and in some corner of that 'accumulated Wisdom of the ages' which is the noblest asset of the human mind find, albeit for the first time, unforgettable moments of pure Truth.

Part One

THE BUDDHA AND HIS ENLIGHTENMENT

I

The Buddha's Enlightenment

The Buddha was a man, by name Gautama Siddhartha, but his place in the spiritual history of mankind is shown by the title which he earned and by which he is known to the world. He became, by effort intensely applied for countless incarnations, Buddha, the Enlightened One, or Sambuddha, the Self-Enlightened One. In the esoteric tradition there are grades of spiritual achievement, and a hierarchy of those who on earth have attained liberation from the Wheel of Becoming. These self-perfected men, pilgrims who have reached the Goal of Nirvana, are known to mankind by many names; Buddhists call them Arhats and Bodhisattvas. But whether described as Rishis, Mahatmas, the Brothers, the Masters, or by their Buddhist names, their spiritual status is inconceivably higher than our own; yet they, according to the timeless and unwritten records of the East, acknowledge the Buddha as 'the Patron of the Adepts', their Master and Lord.

What, then, should be our wonder and humility of mind in the presence of such men made perfect, and even more so in the aura of the Sambuddha, Lord of them all? We must use imagination to bridge the gap that separates their vast achievement from our own. Think of an all-wise friend, with the largest mind, the deepest heart of understanding, the widest vision of the world and the cosmic processes of world-and-man-becoming. There are such men in the world of men, though the greatest of them are rarely seen. If they are not met their words are known in writings or recorded speech, and our little minds can enter the glory of their minds by such an entrance.

Now think of a mind so purified, expanded, and uplifted in its range of vision, and realize that such a man is at most the *chela* or disciple of one of the Great Ones still in a physical body on earth. As such he is still far from the spiritual grandeur which they have achieved. And these Great Ones call the Buddha Master.

Such men, in high or low degree, are living expressions of Love and Wisdom, and the whole range of noble attributes with which we adorn those pilgrims of the Way who have reached the further shore. Theirs is the vision of the Whole, achieved by countless lives of right effort in the elimination of self and the expansion of the selfless Self which moves to Enlightenment. In the course of that journey they suffered torments which we cannot yet conceive in tearing the weed of self from the heart of selfishness, yet, finally, in each, and supremely in the case of Gautama Siddhartha, the self died before Self. The Christ-Buddha-principle broke free of the limitations of the personality, and the 'Thousand-petalled-Lotus' was unfolded utterly. Thereafter the gates of Nirvana were opened for one who had earned the right of entry—and entry was rejected. The supreme sacrifice was made in the full awareness of its implications, and the reward of a thousand lives of vast endeavour was laid aside for the unending task of enlightening mankind.

The Buddha returned to the world of men to teach—Awakening. Buddhas are awakeners, rousing every man who has ears to hear to rise from the sloth of illusion and tread the Way to his own enlightenment. Lack of awakening is the origin of Ill, the cause of suffering, and the only Buddhist sin is that of *a-vidya*, absence of vision, ignorance. The Vidya to be gained is a new dimension of consciousness, an awareness, in the words of the *Dhammapada*, of 'Self as the lord of self'. The Buddha pointed a Way, and about it on either side have grown up the Schools and sects of what in the West we know

as Buddhism. But, as Dr D. T. Suzuki says, 'the life of Buddhism is the unfolding of the inner spiritual life of the Buddha
himself, rather than his exposition of it, recorded as the
Dharma in Buddhist literature'.[1] Thus Buddhism, as he elsewhere says, is the life-force which carries forward a spiritual
movement called Buddhism. It is therefore strange that
Buddhist scholars, in all parts of the world, are so engrossed in
the so-called teachings of the Buddha that they neglect the
study of the spiritual experience which gave rise to that Teaching. Buddhism is a record of Enlightenment and the Way that
leads to it; it is the shrine and should be the vehicle of his
Enlightenment.

Some men heard the 'Lion's roar of Truth' when he spoke
to them in the forest glades of Northern India 2500 years ago.
Some men heard the Message of the Way from these, the
supremely fortunate. We in the West read, in translation, what
others think they understood of that long tradition, and in the
silence of our meditation hear again the splendour of that
Word. 'Thus have I heard ...' murmurs the Bhikkhu as he
attempts to give, in simple language, the Dhamma of the All-
Enlightened One, and we who hear have the privilege, strenuously earned, to hearken and obey.

The Buddha achieved Enlightenment and taught mankind
the Way. Little can usefully be said of this ultimate experience, but much may be written of the Way which leads to it. A
thousand thousand men have climbed to the summit of Fuji-
san to see the sun rise in the distant sea; none told the same
tale of the journey. So we, on the slopes of the mountain of
Reality, learn of the Way from those ahead of us, and pass
to our younger brothers the wisdom learned. The Way
which lies within from its first beginning to its unknown
end is, like all else in existence, twofold. From the negative
point of view, it is destructive, for a man must clear his
building-site of rubbish before he can begin to build. We must
break the bonds of desire, the adhesions of ill-thought. We

[1] *Essays in Zen Buddhism.* 1st Series. 1st edn. p. 37.

17

must cleanse the mind of the illusion of discrimination, the sense of separateness which leads us to imagine the existence of a permanently separate ego. At the same time, positively, we must learn to expand the Self, until this *Bodhicitta*, the Wisdom-heart within, breaks from the shell of unregenerate self and expands into Enlightenment. Does the dewdrop slip into the Shining Sea, or, as the mystics of the world have described it, is it the Shining Sea which fills the dewdrop with the Plenum-Void? It matters not, for the experience is beyond our wording.

With this expansion all else follows. 'Seek ye first the Kingdom of Heaven, and all things shall be added unto you.' He who begins to achieve enlightenment finds that the lower faculties, sworn though they are in fealty to self, change to a new obedience, and for the first time there is a total man to move to his own salvation.

Enlightenment is perfect understanding, and we can and should begin the process now. A positive effort is needed, and the way to enlightenment is to understand until it hurts. The mind must be stretched to include emotions, thoughts and points of view entirely foreign to the narrow limits of our present life. We must understand the mind of the criminal, lie down in the gutter of thought with the drunken prostitute, the debaucher of children, the scum of the earth, for we shall not rise in consciousness to the level of the saint while feeling separate from the lowest members of our family. He who can enter into the vilest corners of the human mind will purge himself of pride that he is not as other men. Then and only then may he reach for the feet of those who do not fear contamination by what to them are still his grubby hands. To expand the heart to Oneness, such is the meaning of Enlightenment, for the Buddha-Mind is one with the Universe, one with the All-Mind from which it came.

But if we cannot now be one with the great ones of our human family, we can induce, by the powerful faculty of imagination, something of the state of consciousness which great expansion brings. We can induce some measure of the cool serenity which comes when the conflict of the opposites, the rival claims of the two sides of the penny, have died away. When all distinctions are glimpsed as falsely imagined, and the essence of 'pennydom' is understood as beyond the use of either of its complementary sides, then something unforgettable has been achieved. The same applies to that sense of certainty, the absence of doubt and tentative experiment which must be achieved so long as we let ourselves be partial and one-sided in our views. We are certain, with a masterly touch in circumstance, or large or small, and in all action we feel some dim yet growing awareness of that rhythm of life which is the universal becoming working through its pure or impure medium, you and me.

The results of even this exercise in self-enlightening are proof that our chosen road is 'right'. Henceforth we ask ourselves, not how much time and energy should be given to the Way, but *what else matters*—save increased awakening? Does this or that lead, or does it not, to further enlightenment? This is the new criterion of action, the sole excuse and reason for anything at all. The ladders to this new state of consciousness are various. Right action is the way of Karma-Yoga; devotion to the Beloved ideal is the way of Bhakti-Yoga, of the mystic of all ages. The intellect studies the opposites, and attempts to approximate more closely every pair until it can proclaim in triumph 'Thou *art* THAT'. Only the intuition, the faculty of *Buddhi* can go further, and it goes so far that it passes beyond our intellectual ken. Here there is no distinction between this and that, nor awareness of any difference. 'Thou' and 'THAT' are no more the ultimates of the part and the whole perceived as one—the difference is extinguished. The intuition functions by direct awareness. It is therefore the faculty of Enlightenment which frees a man from the last illusion—separateness, and being freed it knows that it is free, and is of the substance of Nirvana. If this is to most of us an ideal state beyond imagining, it is not impossible to visualize that nothing less can be the Goal.

The Buddha became, by his own efforts, the Supremely Awakened One. He returned to point out, in the greatest detail, the Path which had led him to that Goal. His Teaching is a Way, the Way to Enlightenment. Then what else matters, what else has the least significance for the pilgrim of that Way but the Goal at the end of it? Henceforth illusion is our only sin, for of illusion, ignorance, is born the folly of our lust. Believing self to be in some way different from other selves we crave for self, and cause our suffering. In the illusion of separation we hate the fellow aspects of our Self. Unknowing Self to be a flame of the Light of Enlightenment, we cling to the spiritual pride which holds this awakening Self superior to other Selves that seem not yet awakened. All this is folly, a cloud which hides the Light, an obstruction on the Way. How much do we want to remove the obstruction, to unveil the Light? As much as a man whose head is held below water craves for air? As much as a man in love wants life? When the whole soul's will is bent upon the Way, when the passion to achieve the next step on the Path consumes all other desire, then only are we worthy of the label 'Buddhist', for then only shall we move direct to the heart of Buddhism, that utter and serene Enlightenment which the All-Compassionate One achieved and offered to mankind.

The Purpose of Affray

Who lives, and living does not find
High purpose in the surge of life's affray?
The unreturning wheel of night and day
Rolls ever on
Demanding larger union,
And moves upon a goal-directed way.

Yet we are wrapped in circumstance.
These gilded bars that margin our parade
Were mind-imagined and desire-made,
And only thought
By which all things were wrought
Shall free the heart by Judas thought betrayed.

What then of dreams, of splendid dreams
Of vision of a newborn commonweal?
Shall substance never know the far ideal?
These present things
Or far imaginings,
Which is the fond illusion, which is real?

I gaze at facts, at present facts
Grey rocks upon the field of circumstance
And yet the very hills shall rise and dance
In joyous flow
And sing as down they go
To dissolution in the sea's expanse.

There's only change, a flow of change,
The rise and fall of thinking and things thought.
Desire and will
These are the builders still.
The temple grows in splendour; then is nought.

The grandeur of the far ideal
Is here and now, and changes as it grows.
And every deed,
The child of love or greed
Is ultimate of purpose as it flows.

The goal, the pilgrim and the road
Alike are mutable as earth and sky
And all are part
Of one essential heart
That beats in life and death, and does not die.

2
Buddhism and the Esoteric Tradition

Buddhism, a Western term for the vast erection of thought and culture which has accumulated about the traditional teaching of Gautama the Buddha, stems none the less from the actual teaching of the All-Enlightened One. But as always men of less attainment took portions of the Teaching and, as it were, encapsuled them in carefully defined doctrine and form, each according to some national conditioning, and there arose, often with alarming speed, innumerable schools and sects. Man being what he still remains, a warlike animal, carried intolerance of differing views to the edge of war, and doctrine right or wrong was argued on the battlefield. But just as each of the schools of Buddhism developed from some aspect of the Teaching of the Buddha, so the Buddha's Teaching was not born from a spiritual vacuum, but was an expression of some portion of that Gupta Vidya, 'the accumulated Wisdom of the ages', which antedates all known religions and will outlive them all. Where then does Buddhism stand in relation to this Wisdom, and who was the Buddha, whom H. G. Wells described as 'the greatest man that ever lived'?

Perhaps the best source for an answer may be sought from present Guardians of that Wisdom, those great minds which are always with mankind, though dwelling away from the worst of its crudities of living. Two of these, known to history as the Masters or Mahatmas M and K. H., answered enquiring letters sent them with the help of H. P. Blavatsky, then living in India, from A. P. Sinnett, then editing an Anglo-Indian magazine in Allahabad. These letters, written to Sinnett between 1880 and 1884, are now in the British Museum, but were edited in book form by A. T. Barker and published in 1923 as *The Mahatma Letters to A. P. Sinnett*. From them Sinnett compiled his *Esoteric Buddhism* which was approved by the Masters as a fair summary of the teaching, and in spite of its title sets out the basic teachings of Theosophy.

For this was the name adopted by the Masters for a new outline of the esoteric 'Wisdom of the ages' to be offered to the West by their pupil, trained by them in Tibet, H. P. Blavatsky. The name was borrowed from an Alexandrian philosopher of the third century AD, but the Wisdom is timeless. All interested in Buddhism as an exposition of the Wisdom should first study this background to both the Buddha and his teaching, for an understanding of it throws a flood of light not only on Buddhism but on Hinduism, and indeed on the whole immemorial Wisdom of the East. Let us then compare these two, Theosophy as the Masters gave it us, and that portion of it which the Buddha, according to tradition, gave to his disciples in the sixth century BC.

There is absolute Truth, which none of us will fully know until we rise in consciousness to its own level, and relative truth, which is all that most of us know *about* the Truth. Of truth and Truth we may learn more from the masters of life, however called, and from search in the deeps of our own minds, but Gautama the Buddha knew more of both than any man in history before or since his time. The Master K. H. referred to him in Letter 10 of *The Mahatma Letters to A. P. Sinnett* as 'Our great Buddha—patron of all the adepts, the reformer and codifier of the occult system ... whose spirit could at one and the same time rove the interstellar space *in full consciousness*, and continue on earth in his original and individual body.' The human mind can conceive no higher man, and for us he is indeed the Master of masters.

Below him in spiritual rank there have been many, though it would be impertinent to assign them any particular place in the descending hierarchy. Founders of religions, Mahatmas, Rishis, Prophets, Patriarchs—how shall we grade them? And

below these men? Spiritual teachers great and small: the leading Swamis of India, the Roshis of Japan, the great Lamas of
Tibet; all these deserve our homage as men who, by unnumbered lives of effort, broke through to the spirit's liberty yet
did not hesitate to dedicate their being to the salvation of
mankind.

Among those who claim to be masters are, unfortunately,
frauds of all degrees, from self-deluded men who, on the
strength of a small experience truly believe themselves to be
enlightened and teach accordingly, to evil men who consci-
ously attempt to gain power over their fellows to their own
advantage. 'By their fruits ye shall know them', and he who
claims enlightenment is rightly suspect. He who accepts
money for his teaching or delights in the plaudits of the public
is even more so. The would-be pupil's intuition should warn
him of the spurious teacher, yet from the current wave of
'Guru-hunting' in the West it would seem that the intuition of
many is not yet fully developed!

Masters have chelas, and many regard the section of *The
Mahatma Letters* which the editor called Probation and Chela-
ship, as the finest handbook available on the needs and nature
of a chela's life.

Such is the hierarchy, and from time to time one of the great
ones comes forth into the world to teach some portion of mankind such part of the Wisdom as seems to be needed at that
time and place. Thus are religions born, not by the Founders
but by their followers, whose understanding will always be less
than the message given, and always subject to commentary,
excision and expansion by later and lesser minds. Some of
these religions are frankly theist, such as Judaism, Christianity
and Islam, and for those still needing the help of the God-
concept no doubt they are of service. Hinduism is at the same
time mono-theist and polytheist, Brahman being manifest as
Brahma, Vishnu and Shiva, and variations of the nature and
powers of these three principles producing a vast array of later

forms. Taoism and Buddhism do not use the thought of an absolute yet personal Creator-Deity.

All these religions break up into many schools, some achieving independent status of their own, and from the whole field come movements which arise from the eclectic tendency of the human mind, each a pastiche or compound of items drawn from many. When to all these are added the new attempts to create religions without any of the usual attributes of such, there is indeed a vast variety of groups of men and women all self-dedicated to some aspect of 'Reality' beyond the necessities of daily life.

Where, in all this, stands Theosophy? As already mentioned, the name, 'the wisdom of the gods', comes from a Neoplatonist of the third century AD, Ammonius Saccas, but the label is immaterial. By any name it is not one of the above religions nor, as too often supposed, is it a collection of items of teaching drawn from all of them. It is rather, as explained by H. P. Blavatsky herself, an outline of the whole system of cosmogenesis, the birth of our universe, and anthropogenesis, the coming of man upon this earth, and its source is what she called 'the accumulated Wisdom of the ages, tested and verified by generations of seers'. It is on a scale which cannot itself be measured, an outline drawing of a cosmic process which in range of time and space, and the grandeur of the principles therein described is in the full sense of the term, unique.

As such it is far greater than any of the religions known to man. Even Buddhism has fallen sadly from the Master's message, although the Maha Chohan himself says, in a famous Letter which has been called the charter of the Theosophical movement, that 'Buddhism, stripped of superstition, is eternal truth'. How much greater, then, is Theosophy than the bodies of low-lit, uninspiring doctrine built about the altars of man's latest gods, Science, Psychology and Social Service?

All these religions have been born, have grown, have decayed and will one day die. So will Theosophy, in this or any outward form. Already the form has been degraded by lesser minds, yet the truth which it enshrines remains. It is at least a part of the Wisdom which the Masters offered in brief outline to the West, using as their chosen instrument that strange and fascinating genius we know as H. P. Blavatsky. And she in turn has given us her own supreme achievement, *The Secret Doctrine*, more than enough for man's digestion in the present century. Yet even the wisdom of those Masters is less than that available to the Buddha-Mind, and that is far, far less than Truth!

How shall we, who choose to study the tree rather than its branches, approach this Wisdom, with what motive, with what faculty?

The Masters, it seems, first teach their chelas what may be understood by any well-trained mind and later, often a long time later, when the selfless motive of the chela has been fully tested, the deeper truths which may never be safely written down. They have said that they influence others, men of good will, to carry out their wishes, but they never dogmatise and cannot, literally cannot, interfere with Karma.

They appeal to the intuition which, when well developed, far exceeds the range and power of the thinking mind. For the higher principles of man include, as we are taught, first, Atman, the Absolute in every man but never his or yours or mine. Atman has no value or meaning for us save through Buddhi, the intuition, which I think of as a built-in receiving set for the rays of Atman, itself a flame of the one indivisible Light. Buddhi in turn, as we develop its illimitable power, illumines the planes of higher thought where Manas studies the truths so revealed. In due course these are reflected down through the 'working mind' and the personality, and appear in terms of use to all of us for daily application.

But note that each must re-find the Wisdom for himself. No teacher can do more than help his pupil how to learn. 'Work out your own salvation,' said the Buddha with his dying words, 'with diligence.' I confess that I was slow to learn this lesson. I could not see, for example, why leading Western minds should not with some humility study the tested and published discoveries of Eastern minds before spending time and money on their own original research. Even now I note with impatience how a knowledge of Karma and Rebirth would revolutionize the range of Western psychology, how some awareness of man's seven principles would speed up research into ESP, into psycho-somatic medicine and, more important still, make obvious that the noblest intellect will never by that instrument alone break through to the plane of the Wisdom which lies beyond all knowledge 'about it and about'!

I see the answer now, and accept it. We must each re-find each fragment of the truth by our own unaided efforts. Only what I find to be true is true to me. In a sense no man ever learns from another man's discoveries but only by his own. 'Even Buddhas do but point the Way.'

Those who wish to contact Theosophy on its own plane, then, must develop the intuition. But this needs study, the full and unceasing use of the higher intellect, for in nature there are no short cuts and no by-passes. Foolish are they who dissipate the intellect, for H. P. Blavatsky herself makes clear that Truth lies at the end of it, and is reached in fullness by no other means. But study is to be distinguished from mere reading. He who would understand these great thought-forces, which is a fair description of the basic principles of Theosophy, must first prepare his mind to receive them, must study them deeply and meditate upon them for hours and months on end. Only thus do they take root in the mind and flower in action. As H. P. Blavatsky said in her Preface to *The Key to Theosophy*, 'To the mentally lazy or obtuse Theosophy must remain a riddle; for in the world mental as in the world spiritual each man must progress by his own efforts.' Add to this quotation the famous occult saying, 'When the pupil is ready the Master appears,' and we know what is necessary for the apprehension of Theosophy.

What do we study? The answer brings us back to the founding of the Theosophical Society, late in the nineteenth century. Members of the Tibetan Brotherhood got permission from their immediate Chief to train the woman we know as H. P. Blavatsky and send her out to offer a new outline of the Wisdom to the Western mind. She was trained in Tibet and in due course sent to the USA. There she met Colonel Olcott and W. Q. Judge. The Society was duly formed in 1875, and in 1877 she produced in New York *Isis Unveiled*. This was, as it were, the bull-dozer with which to break up the cast-iron dogmas of current science and Christianity in order, though the author knew it not, that a far greater work might be built on its foundations. On her Master's instructions she then sailed for India with Colonel Olcott, and founded the present colony at Adyar. Later, the victim of vile abuse and calumny, she returned to England and died in London in 1891. This is not of course, a life of H. P. Blavatsky, for what matters is what she left behind her from which we may ourselves contact, digest, and apply Theosophy.

The literature runs as it were in parallel. Beginning about 1880 two of the Masters, M. and K. H. wrote a long series of letters to the then Editor of *The Pioneer*, A. P. Sinnett, and Sinnett, with a brilliance of mind which is seldom I think appreciated, rendered all this down into a series of works beginning with *The Occult World*. Independently, H. P. Blavatsky, as usual on instructions, was writing her own greatest work, *The Secret Doctrine*, which may one day be accepted as the most remarkable single publication of the nineteenth century. This work, followed by *The Key to Theosophy* and *The Voice of the Silence*, provides the West, as she said herself, with more than enough for the nineteenth and twentieth centuries.

Concerning the nature and value of *The Secret Doctrine* it seems that many Theosophists have failed to appreciate the significance of Sri Krishna Prem's *Man the Measure of All Things*. To a large section of the intelligent public *The Secret Doctrine* is no more than a clever collation of ideas to be found in religious scriptures and similar writing. But here is an

Englishman, a trained scholar whom I knew well at Cambridge
50 years ago who, after 25 years' study and meditation in his
Himalayan ashram, produced his own commentary on the
same *Stanzas of Dzyan*. He clearly had *The Secret Doctrine*
beside him, and in no way differs from H. P. Blavatsky's interpretation, but explains the difficult passages at much greater
length. By any standard of literature this is the product of a
deeply enlightened mind, and it is in my view the most
important Theosophical publication of the twentieth century.
Where, now, is the old fraud who just collected bits and pieces
from others' minds and labelled them Theosophy?

What do these books offer us? In the Proem of *The Secret
Doctrine* the author speaks of 'Be-ness' and its periodic manifestation on the plane of relativity in cycles vast and small. Of
the Plan or purpose of this appearance, and its staggering
range of time and space. Of Man, his origin, nature and place
in the total scheme, and the point he has reached on the long
journey home.

What did the Buddha teach of this? To the public very little
of 'the accumulated Wisdom of the ages', as offered in *The
Secret Doctrine*. On the contrary, he refused to be drawn on
what he called the 'Indeterminates', such as the First Cause,
the truth of Self or Not-self, and what survived the body's
death. Rather he taught a Way, from ignorance to Enlightenment. Again and again he stressed the Way as a better alternative to discussing concepts of the Absolute, or even the nature
of Nirvana. Here is an interesting distinction between
Theosophy and Buddhism, the tree and one of its noblest
branches. Theosophy teaches an outline of the total scheme of
evolution and involution, of the birth and death of the universe
and man. Each Theosophist is left to choose his own path to
this Wisdom, though a Theosophical path can be easily discovered, as I tried to point out in the third section of *The Field
of Theosophy*. Buddhism, on the other hand, began with a full
description of the way of self-development by which the

individual could reach for himself the plane on which alone the Wisdom can be fully known.

Tread this Way, the Buddha said, beginning now, and Wisdom will be found on the journey. As another Master said 500 years later, 'Seek ye first the Kingdom of Heaven, and all things shall be added unto you'. Merely to talk of abstract principles, of first beginnings and ultimate ends avails us little until the self is purged, the mind perfected as a first-class instrument, and the intuition wakened to function freely on this, to us, divinely illumined plane.

Both Wisdom and Compassion are needed. A man does not know the truth until he has applied it; we cannot apply intelligently, helpfully, a truth we do not truly know. And the Way is laid down in the greatest detail, with the Buddha as the guide and visible example of a man who reached its end.

Yet the Indian mind was not content with such a 'limited' field, and in succeeding centuries great Masters of the Wisdom added to what many call the original teaching, and together produced some of the finest metaphysics, philosophy, mysticism, psychology, culture and art of which the world holds record. This mighty field of spiritual achievement does not, however, concern us here. What is more important to the world is the contribution of world-Buddhism to its problems of today. This is the task of the World Fellowship of Buddhists, as also of the Buddhists of the West, of which the Buddhist Society is the oldest and largest organization.

What are Theosophists throughout the world, collectively and individually, doing in the service of mankind? Are they trying to form what their Founders, the Masters, wanted, a nucleus (at least) of universal brotherhood? Are they a body of dedicated students searching for themselves, albeit guided by the Wisdom revealed through H. P. Blavatsky, for the basic principles of the Universe and the powers latent in man?

Both Buddhism and Theosophy in the West have suffered from limpet growths of allied but quite different nature. When I joined the Theosophical Society just 50 years ago I had already read *The Secret Doctrine* and wanted help with it. I wanted H. P. Blavatsky's Theosophy and failed to find it, and in due course, with others of like mind, I left, to pursue my studies elsewhere. The Buddhist Society has suffered from the opposite tendency, attempts to involve it as such in all manner of political concerns, and it is our claim that we have so far resisted such attempts. Let us severally work, as organizations, to effect our several Objects. Collateral activities are for the individual as he can spare the time.

To conclude, the Buddhists and Theosophists of the West, all converts, be it noted, from some other faith, have much in common: *The Voice of the Silence* ('a pure Buddhist work', as the late Anagarika Dharmapala of Ceylon wrote to me, and the Dalai Lama signed my copy long ago) and Colonel Olcott's *Buddhist Catechism*. More important, the Founders of the Theosophical movement in India, H. P. Blavatsky and Colonel Olcott, who together 'took Pansil' in Ceylon in 1880, publicly declared themselves Buddhists and, more important still, the two Masters who founded the Theosophical movement spoke of our 'Great Patron'—the Saviour of the World—the Teacher of Nirvana and the Law'. For them the Buddha was indeed 'the greatest and the holiest man that ever lived', and *their* Master, the Maha-Chohan, speaks in his famous Letter of 'that spirit incarnate of absolute self-sacrifice, of all the highest virtues attainable on this earth of sorrow, the man of men, Gautama the Buddha'.

If there be meaning in the title of this article, may it be this, that all who dare to call themselves Theosophists or Buddhists must study, and teach and strive to apply this garnered Wisdom. In this task our personal affairs have small importance. The bubble of self must be pierced with the sword of Zen or deflated with fresh awareness. In either event the purpose of our dedicated lives is clear. 'If thou wouldst be Tathagata, follow upon thy predecessor's steps, remain unselfish till the endless end.'

The Two Concentric Circles of Buddhism in Tibet

Tibet is alone in the field of world religion in having what may fairly be described as two religions in concentric circles on different levels of spiritual awareness. This is not a case of rival religions in the same country, as with Hinduism and Islam in India; nor of rival sects of the same religion as with Catholicism and Protestantism in Northern Ireland; nor even of two sects of the same religion, profoundly different, living happily side by side, as with Shin and Zen in Japan. Nor yet again, though the comparison draws nearer, is this comparable with India, where the Brahmin caste claims to possess esoteric truths unknown to, and to be carefully kept from, the common people. The position in Tibet is different again and, in our belief, unique.

There has existed in Tibet for a thousand years a complete school of Buddhism, with four main 'traditions', the unreformed Nyingmapa, the Sakyapa, the Kargyutpa, of which the Karmapa now in Sikkim is the Head, and the Gelugpa, reformed and refounded by Tsong-kha-pa in the fourteenth century, of which the Dalai Lama and the Panchen Lama of the day are always members and in a sense the joint Heads. Looking at these schools vertically, as it were, one finds at the base the numerous Vinaya rules of the Theravada controlling at least the higher ranks of the enormous Sangha; then a layer of basic truths of the Theravada; and woven into and enlarging these the main principles of the Mahayana. Finally, on this already complex amalgam there has been laid, and I hesitate to say happily rooted, the Hindu Tantric school of

33

C

Bengal. The net result, from whatever point of view observed, exhibits a wide range of doctrine, methods of meditation, ritual, expository art and mind-development.

The history of Tibetan Buddhism may be found in a dozen standard works. Suffice it here to say that in the seventh century the reigning King Srongtsen Gampo married two Buddhist princesses, from China and Nepal, and the two wives, having converted the King, spread the Buddha-Dharma throughout the land. The indigenous shamans of the Bön faith resented the change and there was much strife, but in the eighth century the great Padma Sambhava, 'the Lotus Born', was summoned from the Buddhist university of Nalanda to reorganize Tibetan Buddhism, and created a school of translators who in time gave Tibetan Buddhists a fine summary of Indian Buddhism. Monasteries were founded with the inevitable division into differing traditions of special teaching and technique. In the eleventh century Atisha, a Mahayana monk from India, founded the Kardampa school, followed soon by Marpa, who founded the Kargyudpa school, his famous pupil Milarepa providing a puzzle to this day of the wicked man turned successful saint. In the fourteenth century came the greatest figure of all, Tsong-kha-pa, truly a Master of the Wisdom, who founded the reformed Kardampa as the Gelugpa Order, 'the virtuous ones', whose yellow ceremonial hats have given them this name.

So much for the esoteric form of Tibetan Buddhism, at one time known to the West as Lamaism. Here is a wide variety of Buddhist principles, deep learning in the vast range of scripture collected in the Tangur and Kanjur, and a succession of high-ranking Teachers of great spiritual attainment. Yet, strangely enough, the whole of this complete religion, of which the West as yet knows only a part, itself functions round the periphery, as it were, of a spiritual philosophy of which the West knew little or nothing 100 years ago. Here, in one sense a smaller circle inside a larger one, is a second group of Teachers, a Tibetan Brotherhood who are of a Wisdom older than Buddhism, each with immensely developed spiritual powers, each a dedicated servant of the supreme Master, the Lord Buddha, whom they refer to as 'the reformer and codifier of the occult system', 'the greatest of the sons of men', 'our Great Patron, the Teacher of Nirvana and the Law'. And these are developed men, not mythological gods. Where their bodies were born is immaterial, as where they live, for not all live in Tibet. In a sense their Buddhism should be spelt Budh-ism, based upon the word for their immemorial Wisdom rather than for the man who last presented it to mankind. But we repeat that their Master is the Buddha, and in that sense they are Buddhists, as H. P. Blavatsky and Colonel Olcott publicly declared themselves to be in Ceylon in 1880. Here, too, are scriptures of immense antiquity, some of them pre-Buddhist; here too are chelas, dedicated and tested pupils able to receive and wisely use such of the Wisdom-religion as they can in that life attain.

Where, then, shall we learn more of this religion within a religion, which is at the same time the root-source of all the religions of mankind? The source is narrow indeed and each must form his own view of its worth.

H. P. Blavatsky, born in Russia in 1831 with exceptional psychic and spiritual powers, was chosen by two of the Brotherhood, with the permission of their 'Chief', the Maha-Chohan, to offer the West a brief outline of the 'accumulated wisdom of the ages', of which collectively they are the guardians.

It was their hope thereby to break the dogmatic theology of current Christianity and the equally binding dogmatism of current science. Further, if this process of liberation were reasonably successful, to re-teach something of the immemorial Esoteric Wisdom with its noble ideal of the common brotherhood of all mankind. The chosen teacher was admittedly far from ideal but in the Masters' view the best available.

As a young woman she was trained by them for many years

35

in Tibet. Twenty years later, after extensive travel and some remarkable adventures, she was introduced to the man who was destined to be her partner in this new and yet untested enterprise. He was Col. H. S. Olcott, and their joint vehicle, the Theosophical Society, was founded in New York in 1875. From New York they were sent by the Masters to India, where they were introduced to a resident Englishman, Mr A. P. Sinnett, the editor of *The Pioneer* in Allahabad. Mr Sinnett, clearly another chosen instrument for the experiment, was fascinated with their teaching and avid to learn more from their own source, the Brotherhood in Tibet. Mme Blavatsky agreed to ask her two sponsors to answer letters from Mr Sinnett with specific questions on the teaching, which was already causing a sensation in Bombay, and the Masters agreed. Such was the genesis of the unique collection of letters which passed between the Masters M and K. H., as they signed themselves, and Mr Sinnett. Between 1880 and 1884 there were other recipients, as there were other Masters concerned, but they are here omitted for the sake of presenting a clear picture.

When Mr Sinnett died in 1921, he left the Letters, and the box he had made to contain them, which is now in the possession of the Mahatma Letters Trust, to his executrix Miss Maud Hoffman, who commissioned Mr Trevor Barker to produce them in book form. The book appeared in 1924 as *The Mahatma Letters to A. P. Sinnett*. A second edition did much to correct the inevitable errors of transcription in the first, and the late Mr C. Jinarajadasa, then President of the Theosophical Society, and I spent long hours together with the originals, which Miss Hoffman had by then presented to the British Museum, to achieve the present third, definitive edition. The fact must be faced that the 450 pages of this volume represent Theosophy, the name adopted for the new presentation of the Wisdom, or at least nine-tenths of it. The writers were the Masters who trained H. P. Blavatsky and helped her write *Isis Unveiled* (1877) and *The Secret Doctrine* (1888). Mr. Sinnett's

The Occult World and his later *Esoteric Buddhism* derived from the letters which were later published in their entirety. *The Secret Doctrine* is an elaborate commentary on portions of a very old text, itself part of the scriptures of the inner as distinct from the outer circle of Tibetan Buddhism, and the same applies to the exquisite small work, *The Voice of the Silence*, which consists of extracts from the *Book of the Golden Precepts* which 'H.P.B.' had learnt by heart in the course of her original training.

Basically, then, our knowledge of the Esoteric Doctrine as such, which will be found to be the basis of all religions, derives from the Masters' letters to Mr Sinnett, and the writings of their trained pupil, H. P. Blavatsky.

What is the function of these Masters, known in other religions by other names but always revered as enormously developed men? It seems that their task is multiple. First, to preserve the Esoteric Teaching as handed down through centuries and aeons of man's development on earth. Second, to check it perpetually so that each generation is able to speak from direct intuitive knowledge of its truth. Third, to teach carefully selected chelas such of the principles as may be fully digested and safely and wisely used. Fourth, to guide (and the law of karma allows them to do no more than guide) world movements helpful to the spiritual evolution of mankind, and to influence, through their intuition, men and women who seem capable and willing to be leaders in this enterprise. Finally, the Brothers form collectively 'a guardian wall' about the Teaching to preserve it from the forces of evil, directly opposed to their own for good. For the law of the opposites knows no exception, and where there is a force for good, a force for evil will appear in some misguided mind whose personal karma in lives to come troubles the imagination.

Here, then, still based upon Tibet, where it seems clear that the grand Lamas know them well but will not lightly speak of them, are very advanced Masters, with their own literature, disciples, and an ever-ready field of work wherein to use to best advantage their enormous spiritual powers.

What, then, are the links between these two circles of Tibetan Buddhism? It is clear that the outer is just one more organized religion; the inner is the spiritual home of a Wisdom, the garnered fruits of unnumbered highly developed men, which can be seen to be the Tree of Knowledge of which all religions are but branches large or small.

Invisibly, there is the undying tradition of such a collective Wisdom, and of Masters, whether known as Rishis, Mahatmas, Arhats, Bodhisattvas, the Brothers, or by other names, of a rank to attain the Wisdom and become its guardians. And this tradition, as I have satisfied myself in talks with some of the exalted Lamas who escaped from Tibet and are now living in the Himalayas, is part and parcel of their religious treasury.

Some of the Masters of this Wisdom are classified in the West as mere mythology. All Tibetan schools know of the primordial Adi-Buddha, and of the Dhyani Buddhas and Dhyani Bodhisattvas and their 'incarnations'. Tsong-kha-pa is recognized in both circles as a very advanced man indeed, but what of Avalokiteshvara, or Amida Buddha, or the four Archangels known elsewhere as the four Kumaras, or Regents of the earth? Are these men who have risen so high that they are now living, intelligent, cosmic forces, or are they cosmic forces personified as, and indeed, incarnate in men? Perhaps it matters little when once the vast scheme of cosmogenesis is grasped in principle.

In literature the links are more difficult to name. Only part of the enormous twofold Tibetan Canon has been translated into any European tongue, and in the *Mahatma Letters* and in *The Secret Doctrine* there are names of works but vaguely recognized by Western scholars. But does not *The Voice of the Silence* rise like a mountain peak above the ocean of mediocrity of most of the esoteric Canon? It was certainly accepted by the greatest modern Buddhist missionary, the late Anagarika Dharmapala, whose life work for Buddhism was largely undertaken at H. P. Blavatsky's suggestion. He spoke of it to me as 'a pure Buddhist work', and the present fourteenth Dalai Lama, when he signed my travelling copy, accepted it as akin to the literature of the Yogachara school of the Mahayana.

More important still is an incident described in Letter 85 of the *Mahatma Letters*. The Master K. H. is writing to the officers of the London Lodge of the Theosophical Society. Speaking of himself as one of 'the Brothers of the Tibetan Good Law', he refers to 'the purpose that we have all at heart, the dissemination of TRUTH through Esoteric doctrines, conveyed by whatever religious channel, and the effacement of crass materialism and blind prejudice and skepticism'. He is concerned lest any branch of the Society should, while specializing in some aspect of the vast field of Theosophy, lead the public to think that this speciality is in itself Theosophy. He therefore gently suggests that within the London Lodge an inner group shall be formed by his correspondent, Mr Sinnett, of 'those members who desire to follow absolutely the teachings of the School to which we, of the Tibetan Brotherhood, belong'. Thus those 'whose inclination leads them to seek esoteric knowledge from the Northern Buddhist Source' would not be giving a false impression to the public of the object of the Society, which included a study of all aspects of truth without collective preference for any. Does this not make it clear that the Brothers were concerned to teach to those in the London Lodge with such inclination the doctrine of the Esoteric School of Tibetan Buddhism, as taught, so far as they were able, to Mr Sinnett?

If these comparisons are of little importance, the unique nature of the Esoteric Doctrine itself could not be more so. This teaching, guarded, repeatedly tested and, ever with discrimination, taught by the Brotherhood, is to be found piecemeal in the *Mahatma Letters*, where Mr Sinnett's distinguished correspondents were endeavouring to convey them to his very remarkable intellect. In *The Secret Doctrine*, which was planned by the Masters, their pupil-author sought to present, at least in outline, some of the doctrines which the Masters thought might best serve the immediate needs of the Western mind.

Here is no place even to summarize the almost inconceivable range of the Wisdom. Let those who want it in a few pages read the Proem to *The Secret Doctrine*, and the 'Summing up' at the end of Vol. I, Book I, Part 2; if need be in the *Abridgement* of the two volumes, where the 'Summing up' will be found at pp. 119–24. But the whole work is a highly condensed description of the coming forth from THAT, as the Hindus call it, of the manifested universe by a process surely of interest to astronomers, for it combines—and apparently alone combines—the present conflicting theories of the 'steady state' and the 'big bang' for that far-off yet periodic event.

It is indeed a surprising fact that there exists no volume comparable with *The Secret Doctrine* of H. P. Blavatsky. In form a commentary on the Stanzas of a very ancient Tibetan volume, with a wealth of corroborative quotation from current literature, it remains unique as a sweeping outline of the whole vast process of cosmogenesis, and the birth, on the return cycle to THAT, whence it came, of that strange being, an animal informed by the one indivisible life of THAT, called man. True, the process is described in a few lines in the Tao Te Ching; in fragments, sometimes sadly mangled, in the world's scriptures; in the code language of mythology, and in the sometimes recorded words of Teachers of but local renown. But the fact remains, that as a clear outline of the total process of THAT's 'breathing out' and 'breathing in' of all that *is*, and of man's place in it, these two volumes are unique.

In her Introduction to *The Secret Doctrine* the writer made an interesting prophecy about its reception. 'These teachings ... will be derided and rejected in this century, but only in this one. For in the twentieth century scholars will begin to recognize that the *Secret Doctrine* has neither been invented nor exaggerated but, on the contrary, simply outlined ...'

Buddhism in Tibet, therefore, in spite of the events of the last decade, is very far from dead. The essence of 'Tibetan Buddhism', alive still in Tibet, is being fostered, recorded, and seriously practised among the 75 000 Tibetans at present in exile, and its finest scriptures translated into other tongues. As for the Masters, who can doubt that they are able to preserve their Wisdom and their work unstained and unimpeded by the passing incidents of politics and war? 'The Truth is great and shall prevail', and those who strive to assist the Lord Buddha in his service to mankind will not, in the centuries and cycles yet to come, for one moment cease to do so.

4

Self and No-Self

It is often said by members of the Theravada school that
Buddhism is based on the statement that there is in man no
self, no self of any kind. In ordinary parlance this is demonstrably untrue. It is of course a translation of the Pali word
Anatta, in Sanskrit *An-atman*, no atman. But there is no
authority in the Pali Canon for such a sweeping statement, and
as all depends on the meaning of Atman in the context it can
be equally true to say, as Hindus say, that there is nothing *but*
Self!

As mere doctrine the Buddha refused to side with one view
or the other. He preferred describing a Way, a Way of life for
every man to tread from suffering to the end of suffering, and
this Eightfold Path begins with Right Views, or the basic principles at the heart of the Buddha's teaching. These include the
Three Signs of Being, facts to be verified by any man; that
every 'thing' or aggregate is in a constant state of flux, forever
changing; that no such thing has a separate Atman or
'immortal soul', and that every thing is inseverable from
suffering in one form or another. Note that Anatta, no-Atman
is a negative. It denies that any thing whatsoever owns or has
exclusive possession of the Atman which, in Hindu philosophy, is the ray of the Absolute Light which the Buddha
called 'the Unborn, Unoriginated, Unformed'. The spirit in
man would be another way of describing it. But it is no more
any one man's property than the sun belongs to any one man
for, as the Chinese Master Huang Po said: 'All the Buddhas
and all sentient beings are nothing but the One Mind, beside

which nothing exists'. Thus no 'compounded thing' (*sankara*) is or has Atman for itself alone. There is the total Light, or Unborn or Buddha-mind, and all things are compound forms of it in manifestation, changing all the time. Thus this Sign of Being should read: There is not in man or in the universe itself any permanent element or quality which separates that man or thing from the totality of the unborn THAT as the Hindus call it, for it can usefully bear no name. This is the negative statement of a tremendous affirmation, of the complete Totality, insever-ability of all manifestation, and hence the pathetic fallacy of the claims of the personal ego to be an important, separate thing.

But the Anatta doctrine as described in the Pali Canon is none the less a magnificent re-discovery, with wide implica-tions for our spiritual development. Indeed, one can re-phrase the Signs of Being thus: Everything is changing all the time and has no permanent validity. This includes man in whom, as honest search will reveal, is no part or principle which is an exception to this rule. The refusal to accept this fact in nature produces, by way of frustration, mis-directed desire and per-sonal craving, a large proportion of the world's suffering. It demonstrates for those still willing to hear and see that the ego is not only an illusion when retained in this form, but a very foolish, pain-producing idea.

But while the misunderstanding persists, and while many sections of the Buddhist Sangha still maintain that there is no self in any form, still less in man a Self, let us look briefly at the subject from two points of view. First, empirically, that is, as we know ourselves, whatever the doctrine of any religion or school may say. Then let us see what the Buddhist scriptures actually say about the self, which is so very different from the parrot cry, 'No self, no self'.

Looking at ourselves, we find, first, a physical body with the reasonable appetites of an animal. Then, higher than this, for we must use some analogy, we have the psychic or astral body, the field of ESP, spiritualism and much beside. Above this is the mind, itself as we all know dual, with its lower workaday aspect and its higher 'wave-length' of the abstract principles of philosophy, science, psychology and the like. All these are suffused with feeling and with personal desire which we must outgrow, and with emotion which we must learn to accept and if possible transmute. Above the intellect at its greatest many of us recognize a faculty which the West is becoming aware of as the 'intuition'. Above all this we must surely assume, if our search has any meaning, the existence of a Beyond, indescribable and yet in a sense the most 'real' of all. And the will, the engine of the vehicle, drives the whole to a given end, and out of our conscious control is the unconscious, at a lower level in Western psychology or a very high level of Eastern metaphysics. No self, indeed! Here is a most elaborate entity, but not immortal in any one of its manifold principles or in all of them together.

What do the Buddhist scriptures say about the self? First, as already indicated, the Buddha was not concerned with the subtleties of doctrine, or indeed with any discussion on 'the indeterminates'. Asked by his famous disciple Sariputta, whether he, the Buddha existed or did not exist beyond death, the answer, however the question was put, was the same: 'Undeclared is this'. And the same with whether or not the world was eternal, and concerning the Self. 'Undeclared' were all of them. What *was* declared? This was always the same. Suffering, the arising of suffering, the ceasing of suffering and the Way to the ceasing of suffering; these were on all occasions once more declared.

We must therefore look to odd sayings, positive and negative, to learn what the Buddha taught about the self. He said in terms, 'There is, O Bhikkhus, an Unborn, Unoriginated, Unformed. Were there not, there would be no escape from the world of the born, the originated, the formed'. But this ultimate Absolute, the Unborn, while manifested in every form can never be the exclusive property of any one of them.

What more? To his son, Rahula he taught, 'Whatever the

form, past, future or present, inward or outward, low or high, every form must be regarded thus, as it really is, "This is not mine; not this am I; herein is not the self of me".' Surely this is clear; in no thing at all, as a quality, attribute or principle, is to be found a self unchanging. And as to the Self, the higher Self as we may call it here, this was an 'indeterminate', and when Vacchagotta the Wanderer pressed the Buddha to speak on the Self he was met with silence, the famous 'Aryan silence' of the All-Enlightened One. But the Buddha explained his silence, when the disappointed enquirer had gone away. To Ananda, his favourite disciple, he said: 'If I said that the Self exists I should have been siding with the eternalists, and if that it did not exist, with the annihilationists', and he repeated, as though it were enough, that all things are impermanent, the first Sign of Being. Every separate self, or the least sense of it must go, he taught, and this tremendous negative was later expanded, by the genius of Nagarjuna and others, into the famous doctrine of the Void, the total Emptiness of any separate thing at all throughout the universe.

Yet even in the Theravada, with its cry, 'No self, no self', there are beyond argument two selves described, as Miss Horner, the President of the Pali Text Society, has freely admitted, and the famous quotation from the *Dhammapada* is enough to make this clear. 'Self is the lord of self; what other lord should there be?' Here is the higher and the lower self of our everyday experience.

In the Mahayana school all the doctrines in the Theravada Canon were expanded to the highest possible degree, and the Self, from being No-self became the total SELF of the Upanishads. But the Mahayana managed to combine the No-self of the Theravada with the All-Self of the Hindus, both opposites being totally true at the same time. All form is void yet the Void is utterly full. Positive and negative blend. There is all-Self and none. There is no-self and there is nothing else.

The Mahayana was a further development from the

Theravada in bringing in the heart to add to the head. For the Chinese word hsin, Japanese shin, embraces what the West understands by heart as well as mind. The distinction which is no distinction is further developed in the utter identity of Wisdom (Prajna) and Compassion (Karuna). The two are one, for Wisdom is sterile until applied in action for the benefit of all, and Compassion is blind without the eyes of Wisdom.

The total man is therefore inconceivably complex. He is indeed very hard to understand, and we as yet know little of him. But knowing as much as we do it seems hard to say 'No self', no self of any kind.

Part Two

BUDDHIST DOCTRINES

5

Central Themes of Buddhism

Asked 'What is Buddhism?', no two Buddhists would entirely agree, but some concensus of opinion must have emerged after 50 years of Western Buddhism with the whole field of Buddhism open to its students. To see what this concensus might be I invited the views of some 150 Western Buddhists living in or near London, to formulate, so far as time permitted, such a list, and the following are notes of what seemed to be generally agreed as a suitable presentation of the subject to a Western audience.

It is interesting to note that the ambit of the principles here agreed is largely that of the Theravada School of Buddhism. It is none the worse for that, for these are truly the basic themes of the vast edifice of thought and experience we know by the name of Buddhism. The Mahayana, though far wider in scope, may be likened to a wheel, where doctrines have been expanded by enquiring minds literally in all directions. Points at the end of the radiating spokes of enquiry may seem to be diametrically opposed, yet all spring from the central hub of basic principles here, it is claimed, set out.

1. The Life of the Buddha should be set out briefly and objectively. Some may not want to be followers of a great man, however great; others may take the line that the Buddha's Enlightenment is the central fact of Buddhism which, unless accepted, leaves the teaching as mere philosophy, far short of the tremendous experience of which the teachings can only at the best be a pale reflection.

2. The audience might well be told in a few sentences what

D

Buddhism is *not*. It is not the religion of India, as is still popularly believed. The Buddha was not a God, but a guide. Idols are not worshipped in Buddhist temples, but the image of a great spiritual teacher is revered. Buddhism is not a religion of despair which aims at the 'blowing out' of the total self into blank nothingness.

3. As to what Buddhism is, it is the widest and one of the oldest fields of thought extant, and embodies philosophy, psychology, mysticism, metaphysics, religion, ritual, culture and art. Although described as one of the world's five great religions, it is in one sense not a religion at all, for it lacks the concept of an almighty personal God, an immortal soul dependent upon the God, and priests whose duty it is to assist this God to save this soul. Nevertheless, the field being so enormous any talk on Buddhism can only be a brief outline of a few central themes.

4. Historically and today, Buddhism is the most tolerant religion on earth, between its different schools, between individuals in those schools and in its attitude to other religions. There has never been a Buddhist war, nor the persecution of an individual for his personal Buddhist views. At Nalanda, the famous Buddhist university, which lasted for 700 years, there were 100 lectures delivered each day by the greatest minds then known to 10 000 pupils, and although we have detailed records of those days, there is none of any illwill or dogmatic arguments between those attending them.

5. The Buddha had, according to the Scriptures, a great range of intellect and learning, to which he added his own unique, complete Enlightenment. Yet he chose to teach his message to mankind as a Way, 'from suffering to the end of suffering' and this way of life, trodden each moment of the day, is of more importance than any doctrine, however subtle or profound. 'The house of self is on fire', said the Buddha, 'burning with hatred, lust and illusion'. When those fires are extinguished there will be time enough to discuss the nature of Ultimates.

6. The Buddhist attitude to life is a balanced treading of the Middle Way between all opposites, including those of the objective and subjective points of view. On the one hand the Buddha exhorted his followers to examine life for themselves, in what is now called the scientific manner, and in particular the 'Three Signs of Being'. On the other, he taught that Reality is to be found within. These, as all other complementary aspects of the mind, must be experienced as functions of one total man.

7. Buddhism knows no Saviour. 'Work out your own salvation,' said the Buddha, and each man treads the Way by his own efforts. The length of the journey depends on the efforts of the individual mind.

8. The Buddha pointed out Three Signs of Being. The first is the omnipresence of change as inherent in every form without exception. The second Sign is the absence in any form, including man, of an unchanging, immortal element or principle which eternally distinguishes that form from any other. If a man's character be viewed as a soul it is not 'an immortal soul', but changing as all else each moment of time.

9. The third Sign of Being is *dukkha*, usually translated suffering, mental illness, and unhappiness of all kinds. In his Four Noble Truths the Buddha pointed out, first, the omnipresence of suffering in all forms of life; then its cause, which he discovered to be desire, in the sense of personal craving or self-ish, self-centred desire. Desire itself, however, is not evil, for it is needed for the attainment of Enlightenment. The third Truth affirms that with the removal of wrong desire suffering will cease, and the fourth Truth is the Buddha's Noble Eightfold Path which he himself trod to the end of suffering.

10. The Eightfold Path begins with Right Views, a deep understanding of the basic principles of the Buddha's Teaching. Then comes the Buddhist version of true Morality, including Right Motive, Right Speech, Right Action and Right Livelihood with the foregoing. Then Right Effort must be developed to provide the will-power to the final stages.

11. The last two steps comprise a complete system of mind-control and mind-development, leading to the threshold of Nirvana. The first is Right Concentration, in which the mind is trained as an instrument which can focus exclusively on a chosen object and then be turned off at will. When the instrument has been created it may be used in meditation, to still the mind's activity, to expand its scope, and to develop intuitive understanding of the Truth which lies beyond the grasp of thought.

12. The universe is the expression of Law. All effects have causes, and man's character is the sum total of his previous thoughts and acts. Karma, meaning action-reaction, governs all existence, and the man is the sole creator of his circumstances and his reaction to them, his future condition, and his final destiny. By right thought and action he can gradually purify his inner nature, and so attain in time liberation from rebirth. The process covers great periods of time, involving life after life on earth, but ultimately every unit of life will reach Enlightenment.

13. The Buddha was the All-Enlightened One and at the same time the All-Compassionate One, for Wisdom and Compassion are as two sides of a coin. The Southern school of Buddhism has for the ideal the Arhat, the 'worthy one' who by his own inturned efforts has achieved liberation from illusion. The Northern School looks to the Bodhisattva, he who has dedicated his life to the service of all living things and takes comparatively little interest in his own liberation. The ideals are complementary. Wisdom is not truly gained until it has been applied in the service of all; compassion is blind unless assisted with the light of wisdom.

14. Nirvana, whether called Awakening or Enlightenment can never be fully described. It is the end of illusion, Reality seen face to face. All sense of a separate self is here transcended, and personal desire in any form is dead. 'The dewdrop slips into the Shining Sea' but retains its full awareness.

Nirvana is achieved in a physical body on earth and in the end 'each blade of grass will enter into Buddhahood'.

15. As Buddhism is in essence a Way and not a mere set of doctrines, all these principles must be applied in daily life until theory melts into experience.

6

The Precipice and the Mountain

The Buddhist Eightfold Path is long and extremely tough going, as all who have seriously tried it will agree. Yet it is complete, from its beginning here and now to its end, Samadhi. Thence the way is comparatively short, to Nirvana, the conscious awareness of no-distinction, no-separation, no-difference between any two 'things' conceivable. All who tread it can measure their own and others' place upon it by tests of which there is no secret, tests of character, motive, spiritual development. But in making these tests we must allow for the vast length of time implicit in the doctrine of rebirth. A child in body may be old in wisdom; a venerable old man but a child in spiritual worth.

The Path seems to have three sections, or stages, although in a sense each step is trodden at once. Right Views implies, it seems, a thorough grasp of the basic principles of the Dhamma, so that these principles work like a ferment in the daily mind and cause commensurate action. Do we live, in brief, as though the four noble Truths were true, and Karma the force to be rightly used each moment of the day? The second stage is the wide field of Sila, morality in the sense of character development, 'ceasing to do evil and learning to do good'. Then, and the place on the path is most significant, we turn to mind-control and mind-development. Meanwhile we walk alone, and yet together; alone in that each 'works out his own salvation with diligence', without a Saviour of any kind save that of the Teacher who 'points the Way'; together, in the sense that 'all distinctions are falsely imagined' and that all things, and hence all persons are alike born of the 'Unborn, Unoriginated, Unformed', as the Buddha described the Absolute.

Now Buddhism, in the sense of the body of teaching and practice which grew up about the Buddha's Enlightenment, moved, as we know, South from its birthplace, and East and North. Then, about a hundred years ago it began to come West. Already a Western Buddhism is in the process of birth, and it may be as different in form as the Theravada, Tibetan and Zen schools are different already from one another. But for the Western mind the Buddhist Path, which is common to all existing schools and traditions, presents its own peculiar difficulties. It contains in particular, and at an early stage, a Precipice; the 'self', the 'I' for which the Western mind so fiercely struggles, in ambition, competition and, if need be, war, must go over the precipice and die, in what is virtually suicide. Later comes the Mountain, the need of full development of a faculty as yet scarcely recognized by science, or even by Western psychology. This is the intuition, known to Buddhists as Buddhi, the inborn faculty of direct awareness of Truth or Reality on its own plane, as distinct from the knowledge 'about it and about'. These two are in my experience the two great hindrances to Western progress on the Buddhist Path. In the East there may be others.

Let us look at the Pilgrim on this Path, who suffers, or he would not take the trouble to begin to tread it. Soon he is faced with self, some aspect of his mind and consciousness which he sees quite clearly works for its own interests at the expense of those of the whole, towards separateness and therefore strife. But if he is a genuine student, prepared to face facts however unpleasant, he will see that the truth of *anicca*, change, has no exceptions, and applies to this self, and every part of it, as much as to any other 'thing'. He sees that he is partly composed of the five *skandhas* (components of the personality), none of which has a separate existence. Yet he is dimly aware, or the mystics of all the world have lied to him, of the

55

'Unborn, Unoriginated, Unformed' which the Hindus have called THAT, and the greatest minds of Buddhism, *Sunyata*, the Void (of all separate 'things'). But for this he would not be in existence, and surely the Path to Nirvana is the road home, the return to the total spiritual awareness of THAT, the Unmanifest.

But he finds in himself more than a bundle of *skandhas* and the dim reflection of the Light of Enlightenment that he cannot yet reach. He finds a set of nobler aspirations, ideals and desires in his mind, nobler than the thrusting, ambitious will to self-aggrandisement, of business, politics, and social climbing. What is this? We can call it 'a discrete continuum of karmic impulse' if that repellent phrase is any help to us. Or we can call it 'character', a more human and helpful term. We can call it 'the Buddha within' still wrapped in the coils of illusion, burning with the three fires of hatred, lust and illusion, covered with 'defilements', bound in a hundred fetters of its own past binding. And we can if we like, we Westerners, even call it 'soul', but this is dangerous, for the Christians talk of an Immortal Soul, and one thing we know quite well of this middle section of our total being is that, like all else, it is changing rapidly and is quite unknown to immortality.

But however viewed, this ego, as the modern psychologist calls it, is utter illusion. As the snake seen on the road in the moonlight turns out to be on closer view but a few feet of rope, so is the self an illusion. *It just does not exist.* All the energy spent on every form of self-interest, expansion, importance in the eyes of men, is illusion, and a pain-producing illusion, for it is this desire, the desire for self against the Whole which the Buddha found to be the cause of suffering. This personal ambition, with its pride, and feelings which must not be hurt, and importance which must be recognized, must be allowed to die, or better, killed. And that which is dead must be watched lest from the dead it rise again. 'Self is the lord of self', says the *Dhammapada*. 'Who else could be the lord?'. But when the Self, the composite character that moves from life to life, has slain the self that holds it back from Enlightenment let it beware lest this desire for separate existence rise again from the precipice.

Yet not all desire is wrong. Without desire in some form we should lack the motive force to reach Nirvana. The mind, a magnificent instrument when fully developed, particularly in a man in whom the fires of self are all but dead, can never make the final journey to the summit. The intellect, and the vaunted Science which the West has built in the field of thought, is learning more and more about the laws of Nature, but life itself, the force which in the end will carry man, its creature, to supreme awareness, is beyond the reach of the microscope or the telescope, and will ever remain so. And even matter dissolves before the scientist's enquiry and is found to be, as the Buddha said it was, just movement, force, changing every second of time. Only intuition, the inborn faculty in every mind of direct awareness, can know Life, or Wisdom (call it what we will), on its own plane, and see that Wisdom–Compassion are indeed the twin aspects of one supreme Reality, awareness of which we call for want of a better term Nirvana. The Buddha never spoke of the SELF, however pressed to do so. Nor did he deny it. He could neither describe the indescribable 'Unborn', nor deny its existence. He preferred to point to suffering, and the cause of suffering, and the Way to remove that cause.

Meanwhile we struggle, each a battle-field of forces warring within, burning with hatred, lust and illusion, and yet in our nobler moments looking up to the light, now dimly seen, of a Beyond of consciousness which, though thought can never achieve it, will one day be achieved. How can we slay the self which stands in the way, and develop the faculty which awaits its ending? We cannot pray; there is no Saviour to hear our call. Surely the Path is the only answer, beginning with the careful study of Right Views, and continuing through many lives with character training. Then with the slow awakening of a sense of oneness with other forms of life, Bodhi-citta, the heart of compassion, will *know* the Reality which lies beyond our present self-ishness. Then comes the first flash of super-rational awareness, Prajna seen on its own plane. However we call these flashes they are beyond description, beyond argument. In that 'thought-moment' we *know*, and the journey is well worth its tedium and self-sacrifice. In this moment we *know* Nirvana to be true; the rest is a broadening process of expansion into the full flowering of that blessed day. But first we go over the Precipice of self, and climb the Mountain on which Buddhi dwells. Good travelling!

7

The Buddhist Concept of Dharma

The word Dharma (Pali: Dhamma) has many meanings, so many that it is, like certain other Sanskrit terms, virtually untranslatable into English by any one word. Law, Teaching, Righteousness, the Norm, all these have been suggested, but it is with the aspect of the term as Duty that we are here concerned.

The basic idea is form, in the English sense of 'good form', or the conduct appropriate to any given occasion. It is at once the teaching and its results, the doctrine and its application. As the former it is Plato's Ideal Form; as the latter it is moral law, the rhythm of the universe. Obedience to the law is wisdom; its breach is folly. Hence Dharma is Right as opposed to Wrong, being alignment with the Law. To the extent that every manifested thing is bound upon the Wheel of Becoming, Dharma is the Way which leads from this to a better that; in human terms, from illusion to Enlightenment.

Such is the chosen term for the teaching of the Buddha, the All-Enlightened One. In Buddhist terminology it is the second of the 'Three Jewels' of Buddha, Dhamma, Sangha; the Teacher, the Teaching, and the body of those whose lives are dedicated to following the Guide to the Goal. As such, it is in Buddhism the purpose, the means, and criterion of values for the treading of the Middle Way which leads to the heart's enlightenment.

For 'Buddhism' is essentially a path or way of life, and this path has many steps of which each must be trodden 'rightly'. This sense of rightness is itself of close importance in the understanding of Dharma. The word is *samma*, cognate to the Latin summus, meaning highest or best. 'Right' action, for example, is action in its most perfect form, including motive, method, time and place. The criterion of rightness is applied to the plane of thought, of feeling and the visible world of deeds, and the actual sense of rightness will be the application of Dharma.

We are here concerned, then, with the concept of Dharma as duty, a duty to apply the Teaching of the Buddha and to apply it in the 'right' way. Now duty is concerned with what we owe, for such is the meaning of the term. It is that which an individual owes to some greater unit of which he is part, and the other individuals composing it. The largest of these units is life itself, the indivisible force whose forms are infinite and everchanging but which in itself has, to our limited eyes, neither birth nor ending. Our duty, then, is to our neighbour, to the community in which our karma has brought us, and ultimately to all mankind and every living (and there is no dead) thing. It is therefore personal, relative and changing. It can never be simple, and is frequently conflicting. Happy is the man who can see one duty before him; more often than not we choose, because we must, between conflicting duties, to different aspects of the life which we know to be one but which seems so bewilderingly many. It is easy to say that the choice, as all action, should cling to the ideal Middle Way, but, as Confucius pointed out, although 'that virtue is perfect which adheres to a constant mean' yet 'it has long been rare among men'!

In applying the sense of Dharma to daily life, there are two factors to be considered, the individual and his circumstances. Both are the children of his own past action. As for the individual, he is the complex product of his own imagining and craftsmanship, from his physical body to his highest or lowest aspiration. His circumstances seem to press on every side yet I, for example, who created mine, have not the least right to complain of them. I who caused my home and job and opportunities, if only by choosing to place myself within their ambit, am still of sovereign will, unfettered in my action save as I have bound it by my own past thought in the exercise of that very freedom. Yet I am no slave of circumstances. What I have created I may, though not as easily, destroy. 'The fault, dear Brutus, is not in our stars but in ourselves that we are underlings'. How, then, shall we choose what is the 'right' thing to do? A study of the law of karma, for which there is no place in the present study, may clarify the law which has produced the present set of circumstances, both within, in the sense of what I am, and without, in the sense of my home, job, family and prospects, for all of which I am alone responsible. According to the Buddhist teaching, the first consideration in deciding duty is right motive. Shall I in given circumstances take the line of least resistance? This may in fact be 'right' but I am choosing it for self-ish convenience, for the advantage and comfort of self. Enter the voice of conscience, the advice of the accumulated wisdom of past experience, and the suffering which wrong choice entailed. Enter, too, a medley of voices from old prejudice, suppressed desires, habit of choice, neurotic fears and downright laziness of temperament. Is there a well-lit picture of the ideal action, and is the will of sufficient strength to drive the machine of self-hood along that way? If so, the balance of operating forces is changed, and changed materially. Karma has been modified, and the net resultant of past causes is now materially different. For I, the actor, and the scene about me are alike in constant flux, and what was 'right' and therefore my duty, a moment ago, is no longer quite so 'right', or it may be more so. For the stream of life, together with its actor and its scenery, flows on, and we that play our parts upon the moving stage must move accordingly. Opportunity may at times be grasped, but the wise man makes it. In doing so he moves from being a plaything of his own past karma, a blown leaf on the winds of time, to becoming the master of his ship of life, a position which is at least more dignified.

What then is right motive in the application of duty? It is

impersonal, a cause for action from which the element of personal and therefore self-ish choice has been purged away. It is a choice made within what Marcus Aurelius called 'the ambit of one's moral purpose', which looks to right causes and is indifferent to unpleasant personal effects. 'Because right is right to follow right were wisdom, in the scorn of consequence', however 'cold' these words of Tennyson may be. The *Bhagavad Gita*, one of the greatest scriptures of the world, is largely concerned with the problem of 'right' action. 'Let the motive for action be in the action itself, and not in the event. Do not be incited to actions by the hope of their reward, nor let thy life be spent in inaction. Firmly persisting in yoga, perform thy duty, and laying aside any benefit to thyself from action, make the event equal to thee, whether it be success or failure'. This action in inaction, and inaction while in action, is basic to all Eastern philosophy, for this alone exempts the actor from the consequences of his acts, whether 'good' or 'bad'. He who performs his duty with a view to consequences must remain, or return in a future life, to suffer, in the literal sense of bearing or enduring, the consequences of that action. Only action wrought from a sense of abstract rightness is karma-less. Hence the saying, the perfect act has no result. In terms of daily choosing, if it is right, do it; if it is not right, abstain. As to the complex ingredients of the sense of right, walk on, and you will learn. Muscles to be strengthened must be used; faculties to be developed must be likewise used, and the sense of rightness is no exception to the rule. But the duty to be decided is always one's own. As the *Gita* itself provides: 'It is better to do one's own duty, even though devoid of excellence, than to perform another's duty well'. By removing from another his choice of action you have robbed him of the opportunity to learn and so to grow. In the end he must decide for himself. Why rob him now of that decision? The motive for right action is therefore to act without thought of self. In the development of such a motive the opposition will be immediate, strenuous, subtle and for a long time effective. 'This is all very well as a concept but what has it to do with daily life? Anyhow it is cold, inhuman and rather horrible!' or, 'It is foolish to get over-tired. Wait till tomorrow'. Or again, 'This is not your business. Why interfere?'

These and a hundred similar temptations prevent our slender impulses from seeing the light of action, and by reason of this quality of dull inertia, in the East called *tamas*, we fail to do what the voice of intelligent awareness clearly said was duty. The pilgrim of the Path must therefore call up his reserves of power. Will is that force, but 'behind will stands desire'. What desire? Is it the desires of the self, for comfort, power, aggrandizement, or the desire for Enlightenment, the sole purpose of entering the Way? Lucky the man whose path of duty is the path of his desire! Said the wise Confucius, 'Better than one who knows what is right is one who is fond of what is right; and better than one who is fond of what is right is one who delights in what is right'. To want to do what one should is indeed a desirable state of mind. Such a concept of duty, performed with such a motive, leads to the 'right' use of circumstance. Things about us are no longer seen as good or bad, desirable or undesirable; they are conditions to be used to advantage as the material of growth.

All of us at some time know the meaning of frustration. If that which is frustrated is the desire for self-aggrandizement it is well that it be checked; if it be the higher and nobler impulses that lack the opportunity of growth, the situation is already covered by the Stoic Emperor (whose understanding of Dharma was so firm and clear): 'When the sovereign power within is true to nature, it stands ready to adjust itself to every possibility that may befall'. Such obstacles are thereafter no longer undesirable. The proper reaction to and use of them is a duty to be performed; we made them what they are and it is our duty to accept and assimilate the consequences of our previous design.

But Dharma as duty is more than a bill to be paid, it is no mere reaction to a situation. When properly accepted it effects a change, profound and lasting, in our mental, emotional and social values. No longer is the treading of the Way a part-time interest; it becomes a whole-time occupation. The Sangha, the third of the Three Jewels of Buddhism, the loosely organized body of monks or temple-dwellers whose lives are dedicated to teaching and treading the Way, are only specialists in a field where every man should be at least an enthusiastic learner.

The 'ordinary man' begins by admitting that some Way of life is well worth studying, and even following—a little way, and from time to time. But the man of Dharma no longer asks himself how much does the Dharma and its due performance matter, but what else matters at all? He learns that only in self-development lies the elusive gift of happiness, and that it is in fact no gift at all. Rather it is a by-product of increased awareness, and it comes to those who no longer seek it. And as the awareness of life as an all-embracing unity begins to control his nobler purposes, he finds that work for others, for the common weal, alone gives satisfaction, and that there is indeed no lovelier epitaph for any man than this—'He went about doing good'.

Dharma, then, to the Buddhist, moves to a central position in his scheme of life. All that is done is done as Dharma to be done, and if it does not advance the cause of Dharma it is ill done indeed. The job in hand, from building an empire to washing up, is the next thing to be done, and the Buddhist does it without thought of self. 'The immediate work, whatever it may be, has the abstract claim of duty, and its relative importance or non-importance is not to be considered at all. There can be no permanent rest and happiness as long as there is some work to be done, and not accomplished, and the fulfilment of duties brings its own reward' (H. P. Blavatsky).

It has been said that all men need a God, even though they change him regularly like a library book. Some men deify Dharma, and the world has known worse gods. This sense of right and the due performance of it embraces philosophy, psychology, religion and morality. It is at once the motive for the Way and the means of keeping on that razor edge. As such the concept is at least a noble means or 'device' (*upaya*) for use while crossing the river of life, to be abandoned, however, as a raft, when the further shore is reached. But whether one adopts it as a God-ideal, obeys it whimsically as the next, though tiresome, job to be done, or whether, as in the Zen technique, one just does it as one blows one's nose, is for each man to decide. In the end there is only Here, and Now, and This to be done here and now, and the doing of it, and the satisfaction which only comes from a job of work well done, the doing of which was 'right'.

Such a new relation with Dharma has its own immediate rewards, whether sought or unexpected. There is a new sense of dignity. No longer is one the sport of life; no longer is life a meaningless and rather evil joke. Meaning is found in all things, for everything is a challenge to one's powers and all of them. Nor can circumstances ever prove 'too difficult'. Shall we who made things as they are be crushed by our own creation? If life be truly one, then all of it, the strength and light and love of it, is ours to enjoy and put to proper use. For all strength comes from within, and the rhythm of life will cure the worst disharmony.

He who begins to live by Dharma, in whom the light of Dharma is a lamp in the darkness of a most unhappy world, is no more troubled with frustration, nor with a sense of wasted time. He regrets nothing save a lost opportunity to learn. In a world where most men drift on the current of a purposeless becoming he is magnificently self-propelled, an individualist without desire for self, an embodied will that moves in alignment with eternal purposes.

For such a man, still very human and with lives, it may be, of old karma to be patiently worked out, there is a new-born realization, a making real, of Epictetus' almost frightening words: 'True instruction is this:—to learn to wish that each thing should come to pass as it does'. Marcus Aurelius put it differently: 'All that happens happens right. Watch closely, you will find it so. Not merely in the order of events, but by scale of right, as though some power apportions all according to worth.'

To the Buddhist this power is karma, the law of exact adjustment of all cause-effect. Thoreau, a poet and not a Stoic philosopher, alive with the poet's intuitive sense of a super-rational Right, sang to the stars his own awareness. 'I know that the enterprise is worthy. I know that things work well. I have heard no bad news.'

When One is Two

The Self is One, inseverable
Unknown to pain or loss or difference;
Unborn of Essence, formless, viewless, void.
It IS, and we of Buddha-Mind should know
That forms, all forms, are lanterns of illusion
Doomed, though born of life, to die.

'Should know'. Who knows? The meditating mind?
It may be that the heart knows more.
The few, whose chariot of will
Has burst the gates of difference may know,
And truly know, and undivided live
The ambit of their days, above
The open wounds of riven love and parting.
It may be so. I am not of the few.
Yet I have known, in moments of no time
When mind is fierce illumined, sudden free
That Self is One, inseverable.
The heart knows more, that dwells in circumstance
And pauses on the swift revolve of time,
Remembering a joyous, foolish love,
Twin pilgrims on the sempiternal Way;
Two that in One were one, yet, hand in hand
Were two in Maya's child, duality.

We loved, the One embodied thus in two.
We loved that, two, had cognisance of One.
Yet I, beyond of mind in Buddha-Mind
Perceive, alone, that I am human still
And sad with severance.

8

Karma and Rebirth

The fact that of all Eastern doctrines Karma and Rebirth excites the greatest interest in the West is probably due to its concern with action, for the Western mind is practically disposed. As already suggested, of the three main divisions of Indian Yoga, Karma Yoga, the way of right action, is more acceptable to the European mind than Jnana Yoga, the philosophic path, or Bhakti Yoga, the devotional way of the mystic. As generally understood the word Karma (Pali: *Kamma*) has three meanings, that of action, in the sense of action–reaction as a single unit, the natural law which ordains that action and reaction are equal and opposite, and the results of action, in the sense of the net resultant of a long series of acts by an individual or group. It is in this sense that a man speaks of his 'good Karma', or points to the 'evil Karma' being suffered now by a group or nation for its collective action in a day gone by.

The law of action–reaction is so well known to a Western audience that the Eastern teaching is best described as the application to the moral realm of the law which reigns in the laboratory. And should it not apply? If action and reaction are equal and opposite, as science declares, why should the law stop short at the limits of physical matter? But if it does obtain throughout the Universe its implications and application to daily life are staggering in range and by their very depth a source of terror to all but the bravest minds.

For if Karma is a living law, the Supreme Law in nature, it follows that luck, chance, coincidence and fate are words to be no more used. No man has luck, whether good or bad, and nothing occurs by chance. Coincidence is the 'falling together' of events by cause–effect, however obscure that sequence, and fate is a term for banked-up causes so near their discharge that no further cause can ward off the imminent effect. Such thoughts, applied to the daily round, are at first profoundly disturbing. I may meet a long-lost friend who is newly arrived from Australia. We meet in a street which I have not entered before, nor he. We greet one another, exchange a few words and part. Was this coincidence? The mathematical odds against it extend to a dozen noughts. Was it 'mere' coincidence? If not, have the powers of heaven and earth for a thousand years conspired to bring us face to face that morning at that place to say 'Hullo'? And what is luck but a label attached to the consequences of my own past action? And what is fate but those effects which now *must* happen? These thoughts must 'give us pause', but which is the nobler attitude of mind, to 'hope' that all will be well, yet to rail at destiny when things go wrong; or to accept the truth that all is happening because it must, that all which happens happens 'right', and all things do in fact work well? If the latter be true then cause alone is of prime importance, and the emphasis of thought is changed from the sufferance of effects to the joy of a nobler causing. Henceforth the mind will live increasingly on the plane of causes, and learn to 'suffer', that is, to endure effects.

A large majority of mankind accept the teaching of Karma, and it is therefore of interest to consider objections sometimes raised against it. Some member of an audience usually complains that it seems incompatible with God. If God is a term for a personal yet almighty Being, the objection is well made, for Karma is an alternative, an older, rational and dignified alternative to the theist point of view. The objection, however, has no value save for those who regard as dogma the existence of such a God. Either the universe is ruled by and indeed the child of law, or it is not. It cannot be subject in part to law and in part to no law, which is chaos. It cannot be ruled by a Being who uses law when he chooses, and yet is beyond its scope in arranging the lives and indeed the creation of products of that law. As a mode of an ultimate Reality the law, itself a living aspect of Reality, is easily conceived, but in a universe so made there is neither place nor need for a personal yet almighty God.

A curious objection comes from those who say, 'It sounds very cold and merciless. I do not wish it to be true'. But the man who, passing a house on a windy day, receives a tile on his head, may dislike the experience while still accepting the law of gravity. He may dislike the effects of the law when it disturbs his comfort; he cannot by reason of his hurt deny the law. In terms of psychology he is applying the standards of feeling, which are like and dislike, to a matter of the intellect, which decides whether or not a proposition is true. A third objection is equally invalid—'I cannot see how it works'. But is there any man, of all who accept the doctrine, who could tabulate the myriad causes of a given result, or estimate the ultimate effects of any cause?

What is the law which so much of the world obeys and has used so widely for so long? Is it purely mechanical and blind? Or is it alive, as all the processes of thought, emotion, and our bodies are interrelated and alive? The Buddhist answer is clear, that there is nothing dead, that all the Universe is but the outward seeming of Mind-Only, and that every part of this 'becoming', by whatever name described, is indivisibly one; one life, one law and one Enlightenment. The interrelation and correlation of an infinite number of causes make for an immense complexity of effects, and yet, as Marcus Aurelius advised, 'Picture the universe as a living organism controlling a single substance and a single soul, and note how all things react upon a single world sense, all act by a single impulse, and all co-operate towards all that comes to pass; and mark the contexture and concatenation of the web'. Life, in brief, is one, and time is a convenient illusion. It follows that the correlation of cause–effect is wider than mere sequence of events. Yet we see the relationship most clearly as a line of sequence, and so long as our lives are moulded in the light of the one eternal life, it matters not that we, infinitesimal knots in the cosmic web, can only handle cause–effect, and further cause–effect, in moulding all things and ourselves just so much 'nearer to the heart's desire'.

⸜ If this be mysticism let us not be frightened of that term. Mysticism is the science of awareness, the spiritual faculty by which the Light is seen, and all its lamps perceived as carriers, dim or splendid, of that Light. If Karma is the law of laws, then love is the fulfilling of the law, and the awareness of the oneness of all life is the link between love and law. What is there 'cold' in a law which links all parts of life in one supernal whole? Truly we are members one of another, and 'it is an occult law that no man can rise superior to his individual failings without lifting, be it ever so little, the whole body of which he is an integral part. In the same way no one can sin, nor suffer the effects of sin, alone'.[1]

In the light of this mystical and therefore super-intellectual truth, it is easy to see Karma as the law of equilibrium, and its working as the adjustment of a balance disturbed. If a pendulum is pressed away it will return with the force which pushed it, and to the place whence it was pushed away. He that disturbed the pendulum must suffer the effect until the force is neutralized in the acceptance, and harmony restored. Between man and man the law works out as love. 'Compassion is no attribute. It is the law of laws, eternal harmony, the fitness of all things, the law of Love eternal'. And the precision with which the balance is restored is frightening to him who leaves his debts unpaid. 'Not in the sky, nor in the sea, nor in a cave in the mountains can a man escape from his evil deeds'. And he is a fool to try.

There is therefore much to be said for the doctrine of 'Pay as you Go'. In this life we get nothing for nothing, and all that

[1] H. P. Blavatsky. *The Key to Theosophy*. p. 137.

we receive we have earned. If debts must be paid it is well to pay them promptly, generously. Thus is the debt wiped out and the mind made larger by the experience. Give always, give speedily, give and forget, whether of money, goods or time. These are not yours, these things, and you will not have them long. Nor does that which now believes that it possesses them, the self, exist beyond the convenience of an illusory world. Why, then, cling to that which you cannot have for long and which 'you' do not have at all? With money, then, give freely, and not for reward. Yet time, when time is valuable, affection if sincere, and the expense of thought and trouble and gifts worth giving, and that which is given to a friend in need, to a society, or even anonymously to one's fellow men, may be the adjustment of a pendulum disturbed. For just as none shall escape from his evil deeds, so none shall escape from his good deeds or his foolish ones, these being labels added to past causes in accordance with our like or dislike of the effects.

Yet this is not 'right' motive for good deeds, to receive due credit at the hands of law. For a man is bound by all his deeds, and remains in the world of cause–effect till the last of them be 'balanced'. All knots and tanglements, all family and social debts must be resolved and honoured. Not till the karmic ledger is for ever closed is a man free from the world of suffering. If, being free, he remains in the world of illusion, and returns, life after life, to assist his fellow men it is that he wills to do so and not because he must. He is now self-perfected, free from the bonds of lust and hate and illusion, free to assist all living things to the same deliverance.

For the perfect act has no result. Where there is no 'self' to push the pendulum there is no self to receive the return, and cause–effect is ended for that doer. When every act has become dispassionate, impersonal, and done because it is 'right', there is no motive in the act, good or ill, and the ultimate aim of 'purposelessness' is attained. Nor is this an impossible ideal. To use a homely analogy, when a man in front of you on the pavement drops a glove, and you pick it up and return it, did you act from a thought-out motive? Or in fact did neither thought nor emotion enter your mind as you did what was obviously right, spontaneously? Yet if all living things so helped one another, without thought of self or hope of reward, in crises great and small, how large the difference to human life, how small the swing of the pendulum!

The law, then, must be used and freely used, and it cannot be 'interfered with'. All that we do is the result of our own past causes, for we are in fact the net resultant of our own past thought. It follows that all that we do, and all that is done to us, happens because it should, and must so happen. The Good Samaritan was not interfering with the karma of him he helped, while he that passed by suffered the grave loss of an opportunity. It is your karma that you should be helped, as you are, or left unaided as you may be, and it is your friend's good karma to have you as his friend. Away, then, with all thoughts of interference. Is the law of gravity disturbed when you hold an umbrella over your lady friend? Yet you have interfered, it would seem, with the sequence of drops of water and the spoiling of her new spring hat.

The avalanche which sweeps towards you down the mountain cannot be stayed. Such karma is 'ripe' for reception, and no new cause of your devising can stay the conclusion of cause–effect. Such karma has the force of destiny, or fate. All else is changeable. There is an old, oft-quoted prayer. 'Grant us the courage to change those things which should be changed; grant us the patience to accept those things which cannot be changed. And above all grant us the wisdom to know the difference!' For most situations may be altered by the addition of some new cause, just as the movement of an object pushed by a dozen men may be altered in speed or direction by the strength of another man. And even when a situation is too powerful to be changed, one's personal reaction to it is at all times changeable. It may be that I cannot stop it raining but I can control, or should be able to control, my physical, emotional and mental reaction to the fact of rain.

Fate, then, in the sense of a force which we cannot affect and can only accept with patience and humility, is a doctrine only true for such karma as is overripe to change. Towards such fate we can but develop the courage to bear such ills as we have created for ourselves by previous action. Freewill and predestination, the delight of the school debating society, are not one of the 'pairs of opposites' but the same truth seen from opposing points of view. Our lives are to a large extent pre-destined by our own past actions, but the force which created those conditions is still free to remould them or to modify them either at the causal or the receiving end.

But if all in the universe is karma-made, then so am I. It follows that I must accept myself for what I am before I can deliberately change it. Having made myself and all of myself it is useless to complain of the body I had from my parents, or of the sex or class or race to which that body belongs. Still less have I any right to complain to an outside cause for any lack of bodily beauty or health or skill; rather should I be ashamed of my own past folly that made me so. But if the personality be self-created, so in a different way is the circumstance about it. True, it was not in this life that I made my body's environment, but it is by law that I am where I am. I chose, in the sense of creating magnetic links towards the whole of my environment, and all about me, body, parents, temperament and job are self-created and must be, if at all, self-changed.

The method of change is twofold, either by altering circumstance or by changing my reaction, physical and mental, towards it. The first is extrovert activity, and all men see it; the second lies in the mind. Thus the alleged antithesis of heredity versus environment is, like predestination and freewill, falsely imagined. I 'made', in the sense that I brought myself into, my parents' body; I made in the same way my initial environment. Thereafter I begin to change my body and all about me, and I change, by all I think and do, my reaction to that changing circumstance. I can, if I think it helpful, and most men do, complain of my heredity and present environment. It is pleasant to say, and believe, that if only things were otherwise I could do such different things and be so different. But it is quite untrue. For those differences would only exist if I made them so, and if I made them so I should be different too. Complain then, if you will, of all about you, of the Government, of your employers, of your ailments and your landlord, of your family, your lack of capital and your job. But as you chose or made them so it would surely be more dignified to change them, if you will and can, and meanwhile to blame yourself for your creation. This is the practical doctrine of acceptance, to take things as they are because you made them so, and to blame yourself, without self-pity or untrue remorse, for everything about you of which you do not approve. Thereafter you may rise, and, if you will, remould the universe. As you are but a flame of the light, an aspect of all-Being, and potentially the universe in miniature, no living thing shall say you nay, and nature will work on with you and make obeisance!

From all of this, and these are drops of water from the ocean of the karmic law, it will be seen that karma is indeed the law of laws, and knows no compromise. Its work is to adjust effect to cause on every plane, whatever the size of the causing unit of life, whether man or group or nation. It does not reward or punish; it adjusts. We are punished by our sins, not for them. He who works with nature flows on the river of life to the everlasting sea; he who resists is broken miserably. But like all other laws of nature, karma may be used.

That which I am I have made myself. What I would be I can be. If I work for the separate self that self will be magnified; if suffering comes thereby it will come because the result of selfish effort is pain. If I work to reduce and finally destroy the selfish self I shall personally cease to suffer, only to find my heart new opening to the suffering of all mankind. For as the self or not-self ceases to exist, the self or faculty of enlightenment expands until, commensurate with all existence, the dew-

75

drop and the sea are one, and the self, the cause of all the trouble, ceases to be.

All action moves towards union, or away from it. That which unites and moves to oneness is in alignment with the universe; that which separates prepares its own destruction. The Buddhist knows no heaven save the awareness of the source of life; no hell but the outer darkness of those who do not know themselves as one.

How, then, does the wise man use the law? He can take stock of himself as he would of his own business. What are his assets, and his liabilities? What is his output, and how could it be more? What stands in the way of further expansion; what new powers are needed to that end? Having taken stock let him re-organize this highly personal concern. Much must be scrapped, of habit and outmoded prejudice; much must be slowly replaced and new attainment acquired. A new spirit is needed, perhaps in the Chairman of the Board; stock that is seen to be worthless, of old beliefs and values, had best be destroyed.

But when the new broom is applied in action the office staff may prove to be difficult. Habits of mind, emotion and body have had their way too long to be lightly given notice; they may, indeed, make strenuous attempts to sack the boss! Creditors will press for payment; debtors seem unduly slow to pay. If Rome was not built in a day a totally new man, converted to a Way of which the end is self-Enlightenment will not be built by a mere resolution. But once the resolve is made there are but two rules for the opening of that Way; begin, and walk on!

It is better to change the reaction to environment than to change one's job, or home, and for two reasons. In the first place, once the mind itself is changed in relation to experience the nature of that circumstance becomes of secondary value. Everything can teach us something; all experience is food for the expansion of consciousness. What, then, does it matter where we live, or work until we have outlived the experience which this environment can give? And the second reason for changing first the mind's reaction is that all about one is the open ledger of one's karmic debts. Be careful, therefore, in attempts to change environment, that the rights and needs of your fellow men are handsomely protected. You have no right to change their lives to your own convenience nor even their beliefs to accord with your own; the utterly self-righteous man who tramples upon his neighbour's will can only bind himself more surely on the Wheel.

Concentration and meditation, regular and progressive in form, and intelligently applied, are the means to self-deliverance. 'Mindful and self-possessed', the new practitioner in the oldest art finds utterly new use and meaning in the day. Was temper the trouble, or selfishness or laziness? The fault is coming under control. Can I see both sides of a question, and even glimpse the plane of thought on which both are true? Is understanding an ever-growing awareness of Mind-Only, and are differences that once seemed as a mountain now stepped over as a molehill on the Way? It may be so; at any rate there will soon appear a newfound dignity. No longer can the mind be pushed around by news or views or change of circumstance. Henceforth the pilgrim is his own creator, his own boss. His desires and emotions may be rebellious and he cannot sack them, but at least he can call a meeting and address them as one who knows them for what they are. Values will soon be utterly remade, and the lusts and longings of yesterday be dropped as a hobby laid aside. With the dying down of personal emotion the mind becomes increasingly controlled and clear, and the birth of the intuition creates the serenity in which Enlightenment is found. With this serenity appears a growing certainty of what is true, whatever else be true, and a rock is born in the whirlpool of becoming on which bewildered men will seek for refuge and not seek in vain. Above all, in the laughter of a man made newly free will be heard the voice of one who speaks with authority, and always there will be those who have ears to hear, and the will to act accordingly.

The doctrine of rebirth is a necessary corollary to that of

77

Karma. If a man is responsible for the consequences of his thoughts and acts, he cannot escape the appropriate results by the death of his physical body. Even the suicide returns again and again to the situation he refused to face until he has accepted, in every sense of the term, the products of his own imagining.

Of the nature of that which is reborn, of the prevalence of the doctrine in the West and the problems which it solves, and of the avenues of thought flung open by this vast extension of the 'allotted span', little need here be said. Books have been written on the subject, and all may study them. But Buddhism, which stresses the futility of speculation, and trains the student's mind to the immediate task in hand, finds little profit in discussing matters which do not lead to the heart's enlightenment. Whether the bundle of attributes which is reborn be called a self, or soul, or character it is, like all else in the universe, forever changing, growing, and becoming something more. It is not an 'immortal soul' which, possessed by you, is different from that possessed by me. It is in fact the product of that which dies, and whatever the form may be, we are here and now, with every breath we draw, creating it.

The value of the doctrine to the Western mind is that it shatters the end-wall of our present life. Instead of a final judgement leading to heaven or hell, or a period of purgatory followed by eternal bliss, which equally offend the sense of justice and the heart's belief, the Buddhist offers a vista of an ever-rising path which climbs the mountain to a height beyond our present imagining. How long that path may be depends for any man on where he stands today and his speed of travel. These are his past and present choosing, but the beginning of the Way is here and now, and Karma and Rebirth are the means of treading it.

When I am Dead

When I am dead, who dies, who dies,
And where am I?
A dewdrop in a shining sea,
    An inmate of the sky?
Or do I rest awhile and thence
Return for new experience?

There's nothing changeless, heaven or hell
    Nor life's oblivion;
Only a heart at rest and then
    A further walking on.
We live and as we live we learn;
We die, and then again return.

Yet who returns, what comes again
    To fretful earth?
I know not. Only this I know:
There is a road that comes to birth
In everyman, and at the end
Shall brother know all life as friend.

9

The Head and the Heart

We read in the papers of a new technique devised by scientists for releasing such power as will make an A-bomb sound like a pop-gun; of philosophers who have evolved an entirely new concept of Reality. These inventions are alike products of the intellect. Do they lead us one foot farther on the Way? Or do they pertain to the realm of concept only, of knowledge 'about it and about', yet knowledge which used without reference to compassion, may utterly destroy mankind? As Dr Suzuki has pointed out, the twin bases of Buddhism are Maha-Prajna, supreme Wisdom, and Maha-Karuna, supreme compassion. The one is useless without the other, for man walks upon two feet. The intellect alone is dangerous, for it generates lust for power, hate of the least shadow of a rival view, and the illusion that it can sometime know Reality. Hence the long history of war between rival schools, and between those who belonged to them, between nations whose leaders fought that a rival concept might obtain; hence the distrust in the heart of the average man for the brilliant, cold and humourless mind that is not warmed by the human, because universal, attribute of compassion for all mankind.

The Lord Buddha himself was no 'intellectual'. Though he penetrated further in pure thought than any man before in history; though he pressed into a single phrase the ultimate analysis of all phenomena; though he was the world's first scientist in the objective approach to all that is, he was, in the application of his wisdom, the incarnation of compassion, and his life was dedicated to explaining in simple terms the Way along which others might, by suffering rightly, end it. Thus he spoke to the suffering Kisagotami; thus he cared for the sick disciple; thus he comforted the unhappy Ananda at the end. His touch was for the common people, and he met them with a loving heart as man to man.

What, then, is the alternative to the intellect? Emotion? Certainly not, in spite of Jung's analysis of the divers springs of conduct in the average man. Yet the triple division of Raja Yoga into Jnana, Bhakti and Karma Yoga applies to all men. We are not all Jnana yogins, those who seek pure knowledge, nor ever shall be. Without its millions of Bhakti yogins, those who develop through devotion to a Teacher, to an Ideal, to a personified Way, Buddhism would have died as a world-teaching in a hundred years, and survived, if at all, as a minor school of dialectic and pure reasoning. In fact, the Buddha-Way, enshrined in a complex Buddh-ism of man's devising, rapidly spread about the world and has satisfied for 2500 years unnumbered millions of men and women whose intellects could never grasp the niceties, for example, of the Twelve Nidanas, or if they could, never achieve their application to our daily progress on the Way.

There remains Karma Yoga, the way of right action. This of the three is surely the Western way, and explains why Karma and Rebirth are always the most popular themes in a talk on Buddhism. The average Westerner is not an intellectual and not, at any rate in England, a Bhakti devotee. He asks of any doctrine, how does it work; and how does it apply to daily life? Buddhism answers him.

Yet deep in the vast body of Buddhism and certainly near its heart, lies an objective, unemotional analysis of things as they are. All things, without exception, said the Buddha, are *anicca*, changing; live accordingly. All things, seen and unseen, are *anatta*, without a separate self. I have, since I first read of this doctrine at the age of 17, entirely rejected the modern concept of its meaning as an unqualified no-self, partly because the Buddha, according to the Pali Canon, taught nothing of the kind; partly because, as I read it, he taught by his silence and in other ways precisely the opposite, and mostly because I reject a statement of fact which every faculty of knowledge I possess, including the intuition, informs me to be quite untrue. On the other hand, I entirely accept the doctrine that there is not in me, nor in any man, a single faculty or part which is unchangingly mine or his, or eternal, or separate from the Totality which men call variously the Dharma-kaya or Buddha-nature or Reality or God. This is a doctrine of enormous value to all men and I believe that the Buddha taught it. As for *dukkha*, man causes it, said the Buddha; let him remove the cause. But I deny that Buddhism is an escape from suffering. The way of the heart, as distinct from the head, deliberately leads into it and through it, until the last drop of 'that mighty sea of suffering caused by the tears of men' is drawn up by the sun of Enlightenment, and the sense of separateness, which causes desire for self and therefore suffering, is no more.

When self is analysed, pitilessly, utterly, what is left to say 'I' and to boast of I's achievements? Nothing. But what is left when the intellect, to its own satisfaction, has also proved the non-existence of a higher, nobler, ever-glorious Self which is in turn unsevered from the SELF which is the light of all Enlightenment? The answer comes from the heart, the impulse in each individual which tells him that greater than man or any faculty in man is humanity; greater than any part, the all. But 'heart' is very much more. The interrelation of human faculties is subtle in the extreme, but just as Buddhi, the intuition, irradiates the higher levels of thought, so does it give point and purpose to the promptings of the heart which, where they argue against pure reason, are so often and so interestingly right. For Buddhi knows instead of knowing about; it knows, and without any medium, the oneness of all things, and the cycles of becoming, large and small, by which that Unity, in a vast field of diversity, in some way achieves its own high purposes.

Its voice and law and instrument is compassion. 'Compas-

sion is no attribute. It is the Law of Laws, eternal harmony; a
shoreless universal essence, the light of everlasting right, the
fitness of all things ...' It follows that the Arhat ideal is
limited, though its limits are for most of us still out of sight.
For the time being, whose mind can we purify and ennoble
save our own? It is easy to choose the Bodhisattva path and, in
the excuse of saving all mankind, to project our own diseases
upon others, thereby saving ourselves the unpleasant task of
rooting out each 'fond offence', and of slaying the self which
cries aloud for the glory of saving others when it cannot save
itself. At some far point on the road ahead of us the two paths
surely join. Meanwhile let us regard the head and the heart as
brother ways upon one Way, but see to it that the way of the
intellect is used for the Bodhisattva way, and does not produce
that apparent selfishness which leads in turn to the state of the
Pratyeka Buddha who achieves Nirvana for himself alone.

For there are two paths, though the Path is One. Head-
learning, 'the doctrine of the Eye', is for the many; 'the
doctrine of the Heart' for the few. The Dharma of the 'Eye'
concerns the external, everchanging world; the Dharma of the
Heart achieves by Bodhi, the ultimate wisdom, the Unchanging. The distinction lies in the purpose for which the Path is
trodden. Whether for self, however meticulously analysed, or
for the whole, however vague as yet that feeling and poor as
yet the power of thought which between them serve the ideal
of wholeness. Between the two we choose in the end irrevoc-
ably; meanwhile, in a small way, we choose every moment of
the day, as the needs of the part or claims of the whole pull
harder. The self wants sensual, emotional and intellectual
gratification. The greater Self—and who would dare deny the
duality and the tension between them?—serves the one life or
light, that indivisible Be-ness which is beyond the range and
reach of thought, before which the intellect, in all its pride and
majesty, falls impotent.

The one path leads to 'the accumulated wisdom of the ages,
tested and verified by generations of men made perfect', those

whose patron and Master is that greatest of the sons of men, Gautama the Buddha. The other path is lonely indeed, and its pilgrims tread it for the reward alone. These are the 'rogue elephants' which, divorced from the herd, must face destruction, though on the way they may achieve considerable bliss. On the way of the heart the rule is absolute, that even the final goal is sacrificed for the benefit of all. Indeed the first step on this path is 'to live to benefit mankind'. This is the path of perpetual sacrifice yet, as is well said, 'there is no such thing as sacrifice; there is only opportunity to serve'. If the Arhat path must first be trodden, because we must begin, as in a way we end, with self-salvation, yet never for one second do we lose our contact with the Life or Light or inseparable Oneness of the Dharma-kaya of which the Buddha in a human vesture was the form we knew. 'Thou shalt not separate thy being from BEING, and the rest, but merge the Ocean in the drop, the drop within the Ocean.' So speaks *The Voice of the Silence*.

The selfish path is much the easier, for on that way lies an escape from sorrow. The Bodhisattva path eschews all happiness, from now until the end. On this Way of the heart all woe, the whole of the world's suffering, is faced and consumed. Nothing of self in the end remains for him who obeys the command to 'remain unselfish to the endless end'. Only the choice remains, and the privilege of choosing; the cold, dispassionate calm of pure untroubled thought, or the ceaseless labour, directed alike by the heart and head, to proclaim the Dharma to all mankind, and to lead all forms of life, to the last blade of grass, into Enlightenment.

Wherever the intellect has spoken alone, men have slain one another since the dawn of time, and striven to bind each others' minds in the toils of dogma. Where the heart controls the head the exclusive claims of the intellect are silenced, and in the silence 'compassion speaks and saith: Can there be bliss when all that lives must suffer? Shalt thou be saved and hear the whole world cry?'

Beauty

Oh, all the beauty of the world is mine.
Devotedly I stand and stare
In galleries of cold design
At beauty pensioned from the world's affray
In pitiless unloved array
Or high on some unhandled shelf.
But there is beauty everywhere
And there is beauty all the day
A loveliness of colour, form and line
Which sings, upon the listening air
Of Self.

Of Self, for beauty, so they say
Dwells in the palace of the seer's eye
And That which views all forms afar
Which made them even as they are
Is beautiful in stone or star
And does not die.

And does not die, and does not fade
Though forms dissolve and pass away.
When falls into the final shade
The cool incomparable rose
The heart of beauty will disclose
Another and another rose, and fill
The garden of the world with beauty still.

With beauty still, yet beauty none shall see.
To mortal eyes herself unknown
Only the splendour of her robe is shown,
Her robes which change eternally.
Her golden train which sweeps the sunlit corn,

Her starlit crown at midnight worn,
The jewelled air when day is born
These are the robes of royalty
And no man's own.

And no man's own. To all is beauty free,
Her scent and sound, her clear unending song.
The sun when clouds have passed away,
The laughter of a child at play,
Home, at the tired end of day,
These to the common wealth belong
And crave no fee.

And crave no fee, but as a lover well content
To see in all things his Beloved smile,
So we that walk this earth awhile,
Of lesser loves made innocent,
May worship everywhere, and in our love begin
To hear, as though some choral sacrament
The soft slow music of the heart within.

10

The Arhat and the Bodhisattva Ideal

There was a time in Buddhist history when the difference between the Arhat and the Bodhisattva ideals was so great that the later or Mahayana School was actually known as the Bodhisattva-yana, as if this change of emphasis expressed the scope and purpose of what, geographically, came to be the Northern School of Buddhism. Yet my own researches into Eastern Buddhism and Western psychology lead me to believe that the actual difference is no more than complementary emphasis, as in the sex of humanity. If this be so, then a study of the difference, its origin and psychological significance, is of value to all who tread the Way. If Professor Jung is right, our minds are so constructed that in certain complementary powers and functions we must needs be more of one than the other. Balance is an abstract ideal, but the man who was truly and permanently balanced would have to stay still, for the act of walking, and therefore of walking on, is itself a rapid alternation between left and right, and all progress is in fact an increasing approach of the 'opposites'.

But each 'opposite' has its own opposite within it. Just as a man and woman have the organs of the other sex still present in a less developed form, so each of the ideals here examined is only an extreme form of a type. Each has within it the dark side of the light, the vice of its virtue, the psychological shadow of its own unconscious equivalent. And it is this 'serpent coiled within the flower' of the virtue which attacks intolerantly the opposing point of view.

It is therefore more than an intellectual exercise to consider the two ideals of the Arhat and the Bodhisattva, to see how each in turn was corrupted by its ever-tempting vice, and to find out, each man for himself, his own particular ideal, why he pursues it, and the right possessed by his neighbour to pursue the other.

Who is the Arhat? In the earlier form of Buddhism, now known as the Thera Vada, or Teaching of the Elders, the Arhat was the goal of Buddhist endeavour, the result of treading to the end the Eightfold Middle Way to self-Enlightenment. He was a man made perfect, for he had purged himself of the Fetters, destroyed the Roots of evil, put out the three Fires of lust, hatred and illusion, attained the full range of spiritual powers and achieved Enlightenment. He had reached the fourth 'initiation'; having 'entered the stream' he had become a 'once-returner', then a 'never-returner', and finally had achieved the state of an Arhat who, being self-liberated from the Wheel of Samsara, need never be reborn. He was, in brief, a man who had perfectly fulfilled his task, who has attained the Goal of Buddhism.

In all this there is, nevertheless, an inherent danger. The whole process is introverted; the emphasis is ever on self and the improvement of self. It is true that in Buddhist practice stress is laid on the elimination of what is usually thought of as the self, but whether the worker thinks of a self to be purified and enlightened, or of a self to be destroyed, he is thinking of 'himself' in its manifold parts, and not of any other. And what is selfishness but over-regard by the individual concerned for the welfare and future of that which lies within his skin? The danger is actual, and was early seen. The Buddha's exhortation to his first disciples was to go forth and preach the Dhamma, to make it known for the welfare and the benefit of all mankind. Too soon the would-be Arhats became self-centred ascetics, concentrated on their own enlightenment, and utterly neglectful of the greater duty, to make known to all men the wisdom which had come to them. As a result, the ordinary 'warm-hearted' laymen came to regard these cold, impersonal zealots as one-sided, lacking a sense of community with their fellow men, with their problems and their several roads to enlightenment. A movement arose to pay more attention to the needs of all men, to the exclusion, it might be, of one's own. From such a movement was the Bodhisattva doctrine born, to restore the balance of a Middle Way from which the zeal of the few had led them into the darkness of extremes.

What, then, is a Bodhisattva? Much ink has been spent on the word's etymology, yet for present purposes it may be taken as a compound of *Bodhi*, Wisdom, and *Sattva*, which can mean essence, being or higher mind. One whose essence is wisdom is therefore a Bodhisattva, but the word gives little of its practical meaning. A Bodhisattva was the converse of the Arhat in that his prime purpose was to save mankind. He was extraverted to his fellows' needs, and his own were of no importance. He was the dedicated servant of all men, and so long as the least of them lacked enlightenment he vowed to refuse for himself that guerdon of a thousand lives. Even the nature of the Goal was expanded, and Bodhi was held to be a far higher state than that of the Arhat who, by his own tremendous efforts, attained Nirvana. Later, the distinction was carried still further, and the older ideal was contrasted with that of Buddhahood, the Arhat remaining fixed at his own salvation, while the Buddha rose higher and higher in the celestial firmament and saved in the process all mankind.

Yet even in this flower the serpent lies concealed. It may seem nobler to speak and dream of a love for all mankind than to concentrate on the ending of the self within. The danger of losing the Middle Way in the darkness of Avidya (ignorance), is none the less quite as great. The Arhat-minded pilgrim argues thus: 'There is a cleansing to be done; the "I" must cease to do evil, learn to be good, and then cleanse its own heart. So shall there be an end to selfishness, and thereby to the cause of suffering. Thereby the mind will be expanded until all sense of self is ended, and it is filled with the Light of Enlightenment.

What other mind can I so cleanse, so expand, so enlighten, but my own?'

The argument is well-founded. As is written in the *Dhammapada*, 'You yourself must make the effort. (Even) Buddhas do but point the Way.' 'Though one conquer a thousand times a thousand men in battle, he who conquers himself is the greatest warrior.' And again, 'Irrigators guide water; fletchers straighten arrows; carpenters bend wood; wise men shape themselves.' It is far easier to fill the heart with love for all mankind than to give up smoking, far easier to 'help' your neighbour to save himself than to root out of the mind 'one fond offence'. The Bodhisattva ideal, in other words, may lead to laziness, to the replacing of hard work by woolly thinking, and the mind's control and enlightenment by the mushy sentiment of vague goodwill.

Both ideals, then, have their purpose and their dangers, their use and their abuse. What is the value of the distinction to you and me? It is this, that all of us are more developed in one of each of the pairs of opposites in human faculty. We are more intellectual or feeling, turned inward or outward, concerned with our neighbours' or with our own affairs.

The first step to the right use of our present talents is therefore to find out more about ourselves. What is our natural line of development, and have we upon that line already reached excess? Having decided on which side of the Middle Way we stand (and none of us stands entirely upon it), we can decide our future self-development. Is it to be by a greater emphasis on self or on others, on inner or outward activity? The answer is for the individual, and the self-answer must be true. Am I running away from the task of self-improvement by interfering, though with the best intentions, in my neighbour's affairs, or am I spending too much time on self-development because I am frankly little interested in the affairs and problems of mankind?

By now the truth of all this must be obvious to the humblest student. It is that neither ideal is better, the Arhat or the

Bodhisattva, and neither alone is 'right', for how can a man achieve 'Enlightenment' who is yet indifferent to the needs of others? Can the right foot go on a journey and leave the left behind? Can the head achieve where the heart is ignorant, or the heart remain indifferent as the vision clears? Conversely, can the genuine and persistent worker for his fellow men fail to achieve the ennobling of all faculty, the heart's release from personal desire, the death of self, the increasing vision of the mind? In brief, we must all be Arhats, working diligently at the dull and tedious task of removing faults to make way for virtues, and steadily gaining control of a mind new purified. At the same time we must all be Bodhisattvas, steadily expanding the heart with true compassion, 'feeling with' those forms of life whose need is equal to our own. Both ideas are needed; neither alone is true. Yet for the time being we must choose the greater emphasis, for only on the higher reaches of the Path shall we discover that there is no difference between them, nor any between thee and me, and between this and that, between any part and the all-conserving Whole.

II

Absolutely Relative

I like maps. I like poring over maps of places I have visited and studying their relation. So with Buddhist doctrine. I like any map which shows me the relation between the 'towns' or aggregates of thought and the rivers of influence which flow to join them. I am now seeking a map which shows the relative position of two enormous countries called, among other names, Absolute and Relative. Where are they, and how does a traveller pass from one to the other? Let us explore, for I weary of carefully reasoned articles, and care not if these notes produce a map to please a scholar, or remain as fingers pointing, however unsteadily, along a Way.

When attempting to climb a mountain one should begin, Zen masters say, at the top, and strangely enough I have found this most effective. So let us begin with the Everest of human thought, the Absolute. It has of course no name, but men have never wearied of supplying one. The Hindus speak of THAT, the Christians, at their best, of Gottheit, 'Godness' beyond God. In Buddhism we read of 'the Unborn, Unoriginated, Unconditioned'. Later we read of Adi-Buddha, Dharmakaya, Sunyata, Mind-Only and the Essence of Pure Mind (or No-Mind).

How to describe this land? We cannot, for it is void of every attribute we could supply; it is without limit or shape of any conceivable kind. All that we said of it would be quite untrue, for to define is to limit; each adjective would make it less as denying its opposite. It is, and that's that. For these notes I

shall call it, with apologies, the Absolute. It will not mind; it
IS!

It is indeed empty of all attributes which limit its totality.
Being total it has no parts. Each part, if any, is of course the
whole. Being utterly empty of any separated and distinguish-
able thing it is also absolutely full. How could it be empty if
not also full? It is no-thing; it is everything. It IS. And when it
manifests it does not cease to BE. Here is mystery, and all that
follows does nothing to reduce it.

So much for the Absolute, but at present I am living in a
country called Samsara. It has many characteristics, the most
important of which is that it is relative. While in it we shall not
see the Absolute; we shall not know the Truth. It is full of
things each one of which is *anicca*, changing all the time. Each
is born and grows and decays and dies, but the life within that
form moves on to another form. My ego, too, is a thing. It was
born (by Desire out of Illusion), and will some day die. Let us
then ignore its existence and forget its tiresome importunity.
And as none of me is permanent—at any rate as the property
of me—we are saved the necessity of salvation, and need waste
no time on our enlightenment, or the attaining of Nirvana, or
other ways of perpetuating 'me' (Hold it: I will deal with that
objection later!)

It seems, too, that in this country of Samsara all is divided in
duality. Each thing has its opposite; nothing is total, and as this
is true it is not surprising that every thing is relative—to every
thing else. We need not, therefore, trouble ourselves with
relative importance. Value or importance is only a personal
label attached to every thing by every person, and has no other
validity. The same applies to approval and disapproval. It
matters not to anyone else what we in our petty minds declare,
very loudly, to be right or wrong.

In this country of quality, of tension between the non-
existent Opposites, we are born, grow, decay and die. Within it
all seems real to us. Mountains and trees, human beings and
their ideas, the things they make and the dreams they dream,

are equally 'true', and our creations, reactions, motives and ideals are taken care of by the law of Karma, which does not concern us here.

Here, then, are two countries, the one I know and Absolute, which IS, and continues to be whether or not there is Samsara. What is the relation between them? What map contains them both? Where is the bridge between?

In logic (a creation of the human mind) there can be none. As Professor Murti rather brutally puts it, 'The two never stand on the same plane; they cannot be related, compared or contrasted'. One end of a bridge can be laid in the concrete of philosophic thought—shall we say on this bank of the river of Becoming. But where does the bridge arrive? It cannot land in the Absolute, for that would be adding something to that which is No-thing and thus be a limitation on the limitless. What then, of this talk of entering the stream to reach the Other Shore?

It seems that a crossing has been made, and is being made, by at least the few. And 'suddenly', for clearly it must be made in 'a moment of no time'. Rishis, Mahatmas, Roshis and mystics of all ages have actually landed there, and have written home to say that they were having a lovely time and why did not their pupils join them? And thousands, including you and me, have had their peeps through the mist which lies on the waters of illusion, and were untroubled to hear that in this land there is no (separate) thing and that it is void of all sense of a separate self which could be pleased with its arrival.

So the crossing can be made, but how? An American explorer said that the difficult takes time, the impossible a little longer. Let us be patient, for we must train for this adventure. We shall need some concept of relationship to help us on the journey, even though we leave it behind, as a raft when one has crossed the river, when we arrive. All religions use this concept, though all have phrased it differently.

The Hindus, who are the most poetic, speak of the periodic out-breathing and in-breathing of THAT on to the plane of manifestation, in a rhythm which, were it not for modern talk of 'light-years', would stagger us with its periods of time. We read of the same process in the Pali Canon as 'the evolution and involution of aeons', and elsewhere, of the 'unrolling and rolling up of the world'.

The field on which this Absolute manifests must be the Relative. Where else could it be? For if the Absolute is somewhere else, it is distinct from the Relative; how then is it Absolute while leaving out so large a part? True, when it 'breathes out' into relativity it does not cease to be Absolute, it still IS, but the relative so excluded cannot become detached. It must still be part of, still Be the Absolute. If Samsara is indeed a manifestation in time of the Absolute it is fair to call it Maya, a term with many meanings, one of which is illusion. And it *is* illusion as viewed by the King of Absolute (or the Council of outbreathing if you object to a hypostatic Person in control), yet all who live in this illusion, this mirror of the Absolute are, as already explained, real to each other.

But this reasoned awareness will not in itself lead us to the Other Shore whence it seems we came. We cannot cross in the paddle-steamer of habitual thought, nor in the jet plane of the higher intellect. Let us then, humbly ask the Wise Ones for guidance. They crossed the river somehow and they must know.

They spoke in similes and parables. They spoke of Awakening to what *is*, of becoming enlightened with a Light already within. 'Look within', says *The Voice of the Silence*, 'thou *art* Buddha', that is, enlightened. I quote this often, for it seems to me as profoundly true as it is apparently reasonable. For if THAT, out-breathing into manifestation, continues to be, then transcendence is also immanence. It follows that each of us, including you and me, has a flame of the one Light within, and must be able to break through the concrete wall of mis-used thought and ego-directed will, and suddenly find ourselves, though no longer concerned with *our* selves, in the Light. Let us accept, then, for it is not difficult, the ancient teaching of a built-in faculty, above the thinking mind, which the East calls Buddhi and the West intuition, but which Dr D. T. Suzuki, who loved to coin these fearsome phrases, called 'intellectual intuitionalism'. This is the power by which we directly perceive, not at first THAT itself, but the flame or spark of THAT which the Hindus called Atman which shines already in every mind if we could but learn to see it. By its light we shall see, sooner or later, the longed-for land of the Absolute and *know*, with a gasp of pure delight, that there is in truth no bridge between Duality and Non-duality, between Samsara and the Absolute, and there never will be, *because none is needed*.

But a single peep is not enough. We must learn to illumine thought with Buddhi, and with the aid of ancient terms begin to see, in the Zen sense of the word, the whole extent (it has no measurements) of the Absolute. For there have been travellers before us who, with the blood and sweat of self-denying effort, and lives of slow deliverance from hatred, lust and illusion, have built up steps, whether rickety ladders or cut in rock, to Prajna, 'the Wisdom which has gone beyond', which is at the same time action in perpetual Compassion, and the end of self-awareness in awareness unconfined.

Meanwhile, between our intellectual knowledge and our yet-to-come experience lies a land of concepts and symbols which none, so far as my enquiries show, can by-pass. For thousands of years men have achieved experience, in meditation, profound thought and applied action, in the field which lies between the five senses and the Beyond. The departments of this country, described in a dozen languages, include what we in English call metaphysics, philosophy, mysticism, psychology and religion, and any spiritual discovery may bear many different names even in one language. In a sense all this is an unavailing attempt to describe in words someone's direct experience, but the phrases have their power and meaning, and as such are the way in which teachers of all time have attempted to transmit what cannot be described.

We must study these terms and understand them, for we

cannot run before we can walk, nor climb up Everest before we can climb the nearest hill. It is useless to be told too soon that every concept and all thinking is but a veil about our 'seeing'. If this were so, then the great ones of the Past were liars, for they spoke of tremendous effort of the mind to think to the end of thought, in order to achieve No-thought. Only when thought is utterly exhausted and transcended in the light of Buddhi shall we know the meaning of Mind-only and No-Mind.

I repeat, in my experience this fog of words and learning cannot be by-passed, and only with the sheer 'guts' to 'walk on' unceasingly shall we learn to understand, digest, and use these powerful and living terms of Buddhist philosophy. And unless we develop the courage and patience to fight through this jungle of dynamic concept, and reach the Light which shines in the beyond of our confusion, we shall not acquire the right to discuss what Buddhism is, still less to compare it with this and that and apply it to the needs of our illusion-laden minds.

Yet the bridge which is no-bridge will not be built with concepts wrought from another's experience. It must happen in our own minds in a 'moment' of conversion, the 'turning about at the seat of consciousness' when we suddenly see all things new and are thenceforth moving, from a thousand different directions, to the same place—home. Speaking of the Wisdom that has gone beyond, Dr Suzuki writes, 'To understand it we must abandon the "this side" view of things and go over to the "other side". The shifting of this position to the "other side" of Sunyata and Tathata is a revolution in its deepest sense. It is also a revelation.' Thereafter we do not see different things but we see things differently.

Are we any nearer Absolute? A lot. By the use of this 'non-discriminative intellect' we see at least the negative Void of appearances, and the complementary, positive 'suchness' of all things, and are the more ready to receive the thundering affirmation from the very heart of Buddhism, not as dogma nor

G

belief, nor with the help of faith but as checkable, usable, cold fact, that the *Absolute is here in Samsara*, that Samsara is in the Absolute, that the map is useless, for the picture of one country must be printed *over* the other; *there is no journey to be made.*

But all this, however exciting, is still mere intellectual discovery. We may agree with Professor Murti, 'The Absolute is transcendent, totally devoid of empirical determinations. The Absolute is immanent too, being the reality of appearance. The Absolute is but phenomena in their essential form'. (May I add from the Heart Sutra, 'Form is emptiness and the very emptiness is form'.) 'It follows that the absolute is realized only in a non-empirical intuition called ... prajnaparamita', 'the Wisdom which has gone Beyond'. (*The Central Philosophy of Buddhism*, p. 321.)

But this is still not enough for the practising Buddhist, who must uncover and learn to use this non-empirical intuition. With it he must learn to KNOW that the Unborn is visible and usable in each thing born, that Nirvana is a state of mind to be achieved in the field of becoming, that we 'arrive', 'achieve', 'become' here, now and doing this. The few who KNOW display their prajna, undivided Wisdom, while they move. No longer in tension between the opposites, and swinging helplessly on the pendulum of choice, they view the revolving rim of the Wheel from the centre, the 'still centre of the turning world'. Serene of mind, freed largely from the tyranny of concept, compassionate of heart, precise yet purposeless of action, they just 'live life as life lives itself', seeing in all about them 'nothing special'.

Well, how do we learn to KNOW that a roomful of this and that is Absolute as well as relative? It is all very well for those who have arrived to say, 'Just stop thinking', 'Just let go', 'Just see that subject and object are both illusion'. How did they achieve this insight? How shall we?

I suggest by building our own ladder and climbing it. We

shall then be more ready for the 'sudden' no-moment of seeing things as they are, in their 'suchness'.

But first we must absorb the shock of the revolution/revelation of thought involved in the discovery. That all this hell of tension, competition, noise and suffering—*is* Heaven? Yes! For some this brings a measure of relief. No more search for the True, no 'crossing to the Other Shore'. No more choice between Good and Bad for 'me' to do. It's all here, in the office, bedroom, classroom, bus, within our muddled, foggy and unhappy minds.

But what a challenge! For there is no escape from this Unborn/born. There is as much Light to be seen—if we open our eyes to see—in a night-club as in a monastery, in a traffic block as in a Buddhist shrine. What, then, must we *do*? We must awake and SEE, by using thought to transcend thought; we must think to the end of thinking, encourage the Light within to illumine understanding by thinking high and higher still, perpetually, all the day.

Such experience will kill the ego-self, and the daily round becomes charged with eternal values. 'Every day is a lovely day', as the Zen masters declare, and it should be filled with the next thing to be done, with the whole man, without thought of consequence. Surely this is the meaning of another master's saying, 'Usual life is very Tao', Tao meaning here what Jesus called the 'Way, the Truth and the Life', and Buddhists call the Middle Way which leads to the Goal which is, in spiritual fact, here and now.

Cease from Running

Cease from running, running fast away;
From danger, change, all suffering;
From death, from time's unloved decay,
From life itself, that seeming fearful thing.

Be still awhile, be still and boldly view
The naked swords of circumstance.
See, beyond reason, born anew,
In light arrayed, bright lamps of difference,

A million things, the blown seed of one Mind;
Thoughts, each encapsuled in cold form
Yet each not otherwise, confined
In bond-obedience to the restless Norm.

Now see within, beyond, and all about
The dark-light of unfathomed Being.
Here laughing Wisdom shatters doubt
And skilful Love in action sees unseeing.

Things. Open them. Cast name and form away.
Here's essence ultimate, unwrought.
Here's present-absence of No-thought
Unstained of meaning, purpose or affray.

Escape? Why flee? Shall fingers leave the hand?
Each thing is part, each thing the whole.
Fling wide the heart and understand
Each self-thing IS, at once the achievéd Goal,
The Road, the unmoving Traveller. Each thing
Is motion absolute, is such
And utterly, a bird awing
Unchained to measurement of sight or touch.

Here's all; it is not other, and in each
The seer and the seen. Then why
This girding to depart? 'I teach
But suffering, until the self shall die'.

Here, now, the refuge; here the unseeming Void.
The suchness of all thingness IS.
Here's Be-ness total, unalloyed
That shines within our insufficiencies!

12

A Beginner's Guide to Zen

The Mahayana itself developed many schools, though it is not easy to say in what order. The Pure Land, which took such root in Japan as Shin; the Shingon which via Peking acquired great influence in Japan for many years; Tibetan Buddhism, a complex form of its own; the magnificent range of mystical-metaphysics, if one may coin that term, of the Madhyamika or 'middle way' school of Nagarjuna and others; and the Ch'an school of China which moved into Japan as Zen, all these and more are profoundly different from the Buddha's traditional teaching to the people, whatever he may have taught of the esoteric tradition to his inner group of disciples. But Ch'an/Zen is unique in being a return full cycle to the Buddha's own Enlightenment. Scorning words and all authority it looks directly to the centre of the heart/mind of the individual, and on a plane far beyond the limitations of conceptual thought. Founded, as we shall read later, by Bodhidharma in the sixth century AD in China, and developed a century later by Hui-Neng and other great masters, it moved in the thirteenth century to Japan where in two main branches, the Rinzai and Soto, it flourishes today.

What, then, is Zen? It is not a religion, nor a philosophy nor a science, for each of these terms implies a specialized and limited form, and Zen is the life which lies behind all form. Nor is it merely a school of Buddhism, for it appears in all religions and philosophies and defies the pigeon-holing habits of the Western mind.

Rather it is the bridge which lies between the world cognizable by the five senses and the mind, and the world of Reality.

It is the spiritual baptism which makes the initiated Brahmin 'twice-born' and which awaits the Egyptian neophyte when after the 'third day he arises from the dead', a symbolic ceremony which was adopted at the formation of Christianity. It is that bridge which lies between the 'lower' and the 'higher' self, the crossing of which unites the various principles of man into a perfect and enlightened whole. It is the final and irrevocable step which every mind must ultimately take, the self-deliverance experience when the weary but triumphant pilgrim moves from the world of ever-changing form into undying life, and happily back to form.

But the manifested Universe is only cognizable to the human mind in terms of pairs of opposites, and all we can say of anything is that it is or is not something else. Between these warring and incompatible extremes the Zen practitioner must tread his delicate way, valuing all things, accepting all things and finally rejecting all 'things' until they are known as complementary aspects of an indivisible Reality. Therefore Zen rejects all theories which proclaim a sole belief in this or the practice of that, or which announce that the body or the mind or the intuition is alone of value, or hold that any one thing alone will lead one to salvation. The follower of Zen regards each single aspect of the Universe as equally valuable for what it in essence is.

Yet if this were all of Zen the seeker after Truth would go his way ahungered still. In order that life may be known it must be presented in some form, and the Zen School itself has to submit to the formulation of certain doctrines to guide practitioners upon their Way. Of these few doctrines, rarely taught as such but implicit in the hints which are given to students, the following are presented with due diffidence as so many 'fingers pointing to the Moon'.

THE UNIVERSE IS THE SCRIPTURE OF ZEN

Zen is Enlightenment, direct understanding, and to describe it in words is beyond the power of the Buddha himself. As Kaiten Nukariya, the author of *The Religion of the Samurai* says, 'The Scripture is religious currency representing spiritual wealth. It does not matter whether money be gold, or sea-shells, or cows. It is a mere substitute. What it stands for is of paramount importance'. And again: 'Zen must be based, not on dead Scripture but on living facts, and one must split open, as the author of the Avatamsaka sutra allegorically tells us, the smallest grain of dirt to find therein a sutra equal in size to the whole world.' It is true that Zen practitioners have their favourite scriptures, even as students of any science or philosophy will have their favourite textbooks, but none is regarded as 'authority' and none is considered as more than a 'finger pointing to the Moon'.

ALL IS MIND
This scornful attitude to the written word is understandable in the light of the cardinal teaching of Zen, that all is Mind, or Buddha-Mind, a self-existent, universal principle which is in itself 'Unborn, Unoriginated, Unformed', as it is described in the Pali Canon. This Mind, or Universal Life alone exists, and all phenomena are products of its functioning. Innumerable stories are told in Zen writings to illustrate the central theme but one must here suffice. Two monks were discussing a flag floating in the breeze. Said one, 'It is the wind that moves'. Said the other, 'It is the flag that moves'. But the Venerable Hui-Neng who overheard them said, 'It is neither the wind nor the flag that moves, but mind'.

MAN IS BUDDHA-NATURED
Man is neither inherently good-natured nor bad-natured but essentially Buddha-natured, although the different stages of human development do not allow all men to express their Buddhahood to an equal extent. Good and evil are seen as relative terms. The sun of our Buddha-nature is for ever shining but the mind of the individual varies as the daily sky. One man's mind may be so clouded with ignorance and its evil karma that he lives in darkness; a wiser man preserves his mind as cloudless as the day whereon the sun shines forth in unalloyed delight.

Applying this doctrine, the difference between the 'good' and the 'bad' person is their relative tendency to expand or contract the inherent notion of self. It has been said, 'All men serve self but their place in evolution may be judged by the size of the self they serve'. The 'bad' man fights for himself alone; the enlightened man for all humanity, and between the two lie all the grades of men. A sense of self is thus seen as an expanding quantity which, like the ripples in the pond, flows slowly outward until the circle made is equal to the surface of the pond. At first it is confined to the personal self; then it expands to family self and so through national self to all humanity until with the birth of Universal Self it ceases to be egoism in the ordinary sense of the term. It follows that there is no such thing as an immortal soul, and that which we call the soul is only our increasing understanding of the nature of the indivisible Self of the Universe.

The last two doctrines are in no way exclusive to Zen, but combine between them a simple answer to the complicated theories on the nature of the Universe with that all-embracing sudden total awareness which is the root-wisdom. The sense of spiritual unity which such an understanding brings to birth in the student's mind is fortified by its application to daily life, which is seen to be no more and no less real than the unmanifested Universe of which it is the manifest expression. We must pass to a doctrine which is a corollary of these two.

TO NAME IS TO LIMIT

As Mr Nukariya profoundly says, 'Give a definite name to Deity, and he would be no more than the name implies'. This doctrine attacks the insistence of the human mind on cramming abstractions into concrete forms; to label, define and classify everything by emphasizing its difference from something else. This exclusive habit of analysis is the child of the lower, differentiating mind and must be steadily replaced by its synthesizing counterpart, the vision of totality which intuitively knows the Universe as one. Much blood has been spilt since the world began over names and labels and outward forms, but is 'God' less God because known by a thousand names? It is to destroy this clinging to forms and names that Zen instructors use curious and sometimes violent means of instruction. We love our limitations, and no sooner do we escape from the confining walls of one room bearing a certain name than we lock ourselves into another with a different name! The wise man keeps his mental eyes upon unlimited Reality and refuses to be blinded by the rolling clouds of form.

ALL IS SUBORDINATE TO SELF-ENLIGHTENMENT

It is a Buddhist commonplace that none can enlighten another, for 'even Buddhas do but point the Way'. It follows that the task of Self-enlightenment alone iş worthy to occupy the wise man's time. Once let him understand that this is already his own essential nature and only one question remains for his decision, the choosing of the means to this Self-enlightenment. These means are legion and Zen instructors make use of anything that comes to hand. No analogy is too curious, no means too strange if only the dormant intuition of the student is aroused to sufficient functioning to understand and develop its own inherent Buddhahood.

These doctrines which are given as mere specimens of a tremendous whole may be found in one form or another in the various schools of metaphysics, religion and philosophy in which the human mind has sought enlightenment. The contribution of Zen lies not so much in doctrines as in the unique valuation which it gives to every aspect of life. There are mystics who concentrate upon the understanding of our spiritual unity; philosophers who concentrate upon the understanding mind; philanthropic societies which pass their time in practical philanthropy, and schools of physical culture which have as their centre of gravity the physical plane. Zen gives undue prominence to nothing, lest by doing so the balance of our complex nature be disturbed. The Zen practitioner is at once a mystic and philosopher, a cultivator of the spirit and the soil, a man of action and a man of thought, and in this contented acceptance of all facets of existence, as aspects of an ever-changing yet progressing Whole, he joins hands with his Taoist brother who, scorning nothing, emphasizing nothing, impersonally performs the action of the moment without ceasing to 'rest contentedly in Tao'.

This balanced vision is the first-fruits of Satori, an intuitive glimpse of Reality, of the sun which shines behind the clouds of form. Satori, however, is usually itself the fruit of Zen training, which in some schools falls into three stages. The first is to be lord of circumstance by control of worldly and sensuous desire. The second step is to become master of our bodies instead of the servant of their lightest whim, while the third is to become lord of mind whereby the Buddha-within acquires the reins of thought instead of being dragged hither and thither at its capricious will. The practice of *Zazen* leads therefore to the death of self and the merging of the Life within in conscious union with the spiritual Life of the Universe. Once more, however, Zen meditation is no extreme, no special matter to be distinguished from daily life. The Zen practitioner meditates each moment of the waking day until he begins to achieve the noble ideal expressed in the *Bhagavad Gita*, 'A constant and unswerving steadiness of heart upon the arrival of every event, whether favourable or unfavourable'.

During the hours which are nevertheless set aside for actual meditation the most curious methods are used by the Zen masters to awaken the voice of intuition in their pupils' minds, but these are understandable when it is noticed what holds us from enlightenment. The average student of the deeper things of life involves himself in a cocoon of intellectual concepts, useful as so many steps upon the way yet, like the scaffolding round a building, to be removed when the building is complete. To break through this scaffolding is the object of Zen meditation, and one of the methods used in Japan to this end is the *koan*, an enigmatic statement or question incapable of solution by the thinking mind but like a ray of sunlight when seen intuitively. One of the famous examples is 'the sound of one hand clapping', and another, 'Where were you before your parents were born?'. In some cases one can give a rational answer to show that one has intuitively understood, but the point is not to find an answer but to realize the truth therein concealed. One cannot truly explain truth; at the best one can guide another towards it, and the whole of Zen is directed to awakening this immediate understanding which no description or argument can ever give.

To the student of Zen the essential nature of all forms of life is its Buddha-nature, and spiritual development consists in removing the veils of ignorance which envelop us. But just as a veil may be torn away or gently shed, so the vision of Reality may be obtained by waiting until the veil be loosened by the hand of time or torn asunder by the imperious will to know. This jewel of Buddhahood is enshrined within each of us, and every school of spiritual development is only different from its neighbour in the means employed towards this end. The Zen school scorns ascetic practices or too much thought, and uses, in daily life, any and every means which rouses the dormant Buddhahood to conscious functioning. The most trivial incidents no less display the workings of eternal law than the grandeur of the heavens; while a sudden phrase or movement or even blow may startle the keen pursuer of truth from the conventional rut of prejudice and limiting convictions, of logical analysis and rational thought, to 'see'.

Zen is therefore at once Enlightenment and the Way that leads to it. It never explains, it merely indicates. It says but little but it points the Way. It is the factor which keeps a religion vital, in the absence of which it petrifies and dies. There is nothing curious or unnatural about it. It is the simplest and most natural process of all, a deliberate alignment of one's inner self with that movement which is life, the life-stream of the Universe, and an understanding of its nature gathered on the way. Stop to argue and consider, and you find that life has flowed away from you. Only the dry bones of doctrines and ideas remain. At-one your life with all the Universe and therein you find Enlightenment.

Books are the bones of Buddhism. Zen is its heart.

13

Soto Zen

We now have a wide knowledge of Rinzai Zen Buddhism, but of Soto Zen, which as a school is of equal age, and claims today a larger number of followers in Japan, we still know comparatively little. One reason is, of course, that the late Dr D. T. Suzuki, who gained his enlightenment in the Rinzai Zen school, wrote of it almost exclusively, and the literature of Zen in Europe is still largely Rinzai Zen. There is, on the other hand, a paucity of literature on the subject of Soto Zen, and Professor Masunaga's *The Soto Approach to Zen*, translating part of the most famous of the writings of Dogen, the founder of the school in Japan, remains the standard source of information for the West. Yet Dogen (1200 to 1253) was a very great man, the greatest mind which has appeared in Japanese Buddhism until modern times. True, his writings stand at a very high level of awareness, comparable with the greatest minds which created the literature of the *Prajna-paramita*, 'the Wisdom which has gone Beyond', but one would expect more Western students to be striving for that awareness. As the Soto Zen school developed in Japan it seems to have been influenced by the parallel development of the Shin or Pure Land school, associated with the names of Honen and Shinran Shonin. Certainly there seem to be affinities between the two, and they resemble each other noticeably when found in countries outside Japan. It is therefore surprising that Western students of Zen who have found the Rinzai school too violent should still be indifferent to the Soto school, which stands between the two extremes of Zen and Shin.

The history of the two sects runs side by side. It was Bodhidharma, a Buddhist from South India who about AD 500 brought what we now call Zen Buddhism from India to China. By the time of Hui-neng (638–713), known in Japan as Eno, this Ch'an (Zen) Buddhism was well established as a school, though still bearing traces of its Indian origin. Throughout this period of 200 years the emphasis was on Dhyana, meditation, rather than on Prajna, wisdom, in the sense of supreme Wisdom 'suddenly' attained. Hui-neng fused the two into wisdom practised in meditation, but he, the sixth Patriarch, left no successor. His School inevitably split up, and was soon in five 'Houses' or sub-divisions, the details of which may be seen in Chapter II of *The Development of Chinese Zen* (Dumoulin and Sasaki), and the valuable charts at the end of it. Of these schools the most important were the progenitors of the Rinzai and Soto schools of Japan. Each descended from a pupil of Hui-neng, the Soto through Ungan, Tosan and Wanshi to the Japanese Dogen.

As is always the process where two masters differ on relative emphasis, even if no more, the split widened, and by the twelfth century Daie Soko (a pupil of Engo, the subject of the Hekigan-roku) had systematized the koan practice into 'Kanna' Zen, while the Soto School under Wanshi favoured 'Mokusho' Zen, the quiet sitting in zazen in which enlightenment, insight into the Void, is attained without the use of the koan and mondo technique. It may be that the Rinzai emphasis on the koan came about with a decline of the great masters who needed no technique of any kind, but without this quantum of system in the training it is doubtful if Rinzai Zen, with its enormous effect on the spiritual culture of Japan, would have survived.

It was Dogen who brought the Soto teachings from China to Japan, about the time that Eisai (1141–1215) brought over the Rinzai school, but whereas other scholars brought increasing knowledge of the latter teaching, Dogen stands alone as the founder of Soto Zen in Japan. He actually studied under Eisai, but at the age of 24 crossed to China, where he studied for four years and gained his enlightenment. On his return to Japan he would have no dealings with the Court, nor with worldly affairs in any form. He trained his followers to meditate in za-zen, and to blend an increasing inner awareness of the Buddha-within with the practice of high morality and compassion for all. For him the sitting, the moral training and the Buddha-Enlightenment were three facets of one practice. Unlike most great men of the past, he wrote down his teaching, of which the most famous is the *Shobogenzo*, the Eye of the True Law, from which Dr Masunaga has translated the sections known as Genjokoan, Uji, Shoji and Bendowa. There is in it a blend of the traditional and the personal. Dogen's attitude to the past was to attempt to reduce the process of splitting Buddhism into more and more sects, and to restore the main tradition of the Buddha's own direct path to Enlightenment.

First, he taught, abandon outward observance in favour of realizing the Buddha within. As he wrote in his great work, 'The burning of incense, the bowing before the Buddha's image and prayer to him, confession of sin and the reading of the Sutras are all, from the very beginning of one's discipleship, wholly unnecessary. The one and only thing required is to free oneself from the bondage of mind and body alike, putting the Buddha's own seal upon yourself. If you do this as you sit in ecstatic meditation the whole universe itself turns into enlightenment. This is what I mean by the Buddha's seal'.

By emptying the heart of self we make room for the Buddha, who is, however, already enthroned. Dr Suzuki writes that when Dogen returned from China he was asked what he had learned. He said, 'Not much except *nyunanshin*!' which the writer translates as 'gentleness of spirit'. 'Generally', is Dr Suzuki's comment, 'we are too egoistic, too full of hard, resisting spirit. We are individualistic, unable to accept things as they are or as they come to us. Resistance means friction, friction is the source of all trouble. When there is no-self the heart is soft and offers no resistance to outside influences. This does not mean the absence of all sensitivities or emotionalities. They are controlled in the totality of a spiritual outlook on life.'

If we are all and each of us Buddha why not act accordingly? Let us act each moment of the day *as if* we were, what in fact we are, enlightened beings. And the only right moment of action is now. The past and the future are unimportant. There is only now. 'If life comes, this is life. If death comes, this is death. There is no reason for your being under their control.'

This teaching calls for faith, that we are already enlightened. But, as writers on Soto Zen point out, every religion calls for faith, and even the least religious of Buddhist Schools, the Theravada, implies the existence of faith in the fact of the Buddha's Enlightenment. Add to this belief a life lived *as if* the Buddha were actually living within, and mere faith becomes true spiritual knowledge. But this faith was never allowed to degenerate to the level of the 'nembutsu' of the Shin or Pure Land School. In the Bendowa section of the Shobogenzo we read, 'What good are such actions as reading the sutras and saying the nembutsu? How futile to think that merits accrue from merely moving the tongue and raising the voice! If you think this covers Buddhism you are far from the truth. Constant repetition of the nembutsu is worthless, like a frog in a spring field croaking night and day'.

But with faith developed and applied the novice may set to work. First, with repentance, which figures largely. Dr Hunt, an Englishman who founded a school of Soto Zen in Honolulu, quotes a Soto saying, 'In the shadow of repentance there lies satori'. For repentance has a double value, to purge the mind of the errors which caused our present sins, and to strengthen it for a swifter approach to awareness of our indwelling Buddhahood.

And so to the practice of za-zen, or Zen sitting. In Rinzai Zen this is meditation with a koan or mondo as 'seed'; in Soto Zen it is not a way leading to Enlightenment but a religious practice carried on in a state of Enlightenment. It is training based on enlightenment, the training and the state being inseverable. Dogen's za-zen is not a means to an end but the end in itself. It is cross-legged sitting with no gain and no expectation—a way of living in one's own true self. Since truly transmitted za-zen is superior training enfolding original enlightenment, it frees itself from the wait for enlightenment and the wish to become a Buddha. The idea is to live daily in the spirit of meditation, whether in working, playing or in resting. In other words, life is the active expression of Buddha at work.

These collated quotations show the nature and no-purpose of Soto Zen meditation, but they hint at the supreme importance of the master as the 'true transmitter' of correct za-zen. The master–pupil relationship is so close that their minds are interdiffused, and in the end the disciple has to transcend the master.

The za-zen in the Zendo, or meditation hall, is applied each moment of the day in 16 precepts, which are a collection of lists from the Theravada School, consisting of the Three Refuges; the well-known three components of the Buddhist life, 'Cease to do evil. Learn to do good. Cleanse your own heart', and a new version of the Ten Precepts. The last factor in the teaching, the strict observance of ritual, is somewhat surprising, and was surprising to me when I was privileged to spend a night and a day with the monks of Sojiji, near Tokyo. Zen and ritual seem far apart, but this is no place to consider how in fact the blinkers of ritual may keep the mind one-pointed on its object of No-object.

Comparison between the schools is inevitable. Historically, Dogen, who alone brought the Soto School to Japan, avoided the Court and politics, and kept to the mountains and the people of humble stock. Rinzai Zen was early taken up by the Court and the warriors, and was soon incorporated in Bushido, the samurai cult of the sword. While the scriptures used by Rinzai are the wide field of Chinese texts and those

113

H

translated from the Sanskrit, the followers of Dogen use but his own writings. In terms of technique, the Rinzai School uses the koan and mondo; the Soto School affects to despise them as leading but to an artificial satori, but I understand that many of the Soto masters of today were in fact Rinzai-trained. The distinction between sudden and gradual enlightenment is, I believe, untrue; the moment when it comes is always sudden, but the preparation for it, even of no-preparation, is always long. If the one is more warrior-like, 'storming the gates of Heaven', and the other more Taoist and pregnant of wu-wei; if one is more extravert, seeking the infinite in finite things, and the other more gently mystical, these are distinctions with little difference. The Rinzai goes straight for Prajna, dynamic Wisdom; Soto quietism is content with Dhyana, meditation. But Karuna, compassion, is the use of Prajna, and Wisdom is its source. So long as there is male and female, night and day, there will be comparative emphasis in all technique. Both these Schools are sub-schools of one group of minds that strive to return directly to the Buddha's own Enlightenment. The means to the end must vary with the pilgrim; the mountain and the task are one.

Part Three

BUDDHISM COMES WEST

14

Buddhism comes West

Buddhism is a collection of doctrines which contains the widest field of human thought yet attained by man. No other religion has its range of metaphysics, philosophy, mysticism, psychology, religious practice, mind-development, culture and art. Historically, it stems from the spiritual achievement of one man in North-East India, on a date, of remarkably little consequence to the practising Buddhist, in the fifth–sixth century BC. Its fundamental premise, alone to be accepted 'on faith', is that the Enlightenment claimed by the Buddha is achievable by all men, and here on earth.

The Buddha proclaimed to his disciples and to the common people a Way, the path trodden by himself from ignorance to enlightenment, from self to the end of a separate self, in the state of consciousness in Pali called Nibbana. After his passing, Councils were held to discuss and if possible to agree on his Teaching, but the human mind is highly complex, and very soon differences of emphasis and way of interpretation began to appear. Although there was general agreement on basic principles, a series of complementary doctrines soon reached formulation, and those who favoured them found themselves in different schools whose doctrines and practices acquired a collective name and Canon. These new developments, I believe, were inevitable, for they reflected the complementary aspect of the human mind.

The Buddha may have limited his public teaching to 'suffering and release from suffering' achieved by a well-mapped Way, but the greatest minds of India were not content with such a simple teaching, and sought and found new avenues of mind-development into the highest levels of consciousness achieved by man. In the thousand years which followed the Buddha's passing, men of the highest mental status achieved for themselves their measure of enlightenment, and in the *Prajna-paramita* literature, for example, wrote what can be written of this experience.

Meanwhile, what seems to be the oldest school of Buddhism, the Theravada, which alone survived of the 18 sub-divisions of the Hinayana, was firmly established and flourishes today in Sri Lanka, Burma and Thailand. Yet in terms of numbers and geographical area the Theravada covers less than half the Buddhist field, for the Dhamma was carried East, to China, Korea and Japan, North into Tibet and Mongolia, and the expanded teaching known as the Mahayana was at one time a powerful factor in a thousand million minds. As such it existed in a dozen different forms, and while each of these traditions was content with its own teaching, scriptures and methods of meditation, it was no one's business to compare them or to record the common ground.

Then came the world example of the University of Nalanda, in which, a traveller tells us, there were in the seventh century 10 000 students living in harmony, lectured to by a hundred of the finest minds of the day on all the then known lines of Buddhist thought-development. Here was more than negative tolerance, in the sense of an absence of intolerance of a differing point of view; here for 700 years was eager comparison of thought and thought-achievement. Surely this should be an example to us all today of 'world Buddhism' in theory, ready to become world Buddhism in action as each of the Nalanda students, complete with awareness of the total Buddhist field, returned home.

So much for the dispersal of the Doctrine, and an historic example of its reintegration for the mutual benefit of all. By AD 1200 Buddhism as such had been driven from India, and the field elsewhere was almost static. The Theravada produced no great thinker or writer after Buddhagosha, and was content to preserve the Dhamma in the form in which it began to be written down about 100 BC. There were minor developments and movements of reform in several countries of the Mahayana, with some schools dying and others being born, but there was no substantial change for the next 700 years, during which time each school was hardened in its own ideas and practices.

In the nineteenth century a new ferment appeared which in the last 80 years has worked with increasing rapidity. In India the pioneering force was that remarkable man, the late Anagarika Dharmapala. Thanks to his untiring efforts the Maha Bodhi Society was born, and for 60 years has worked to bring Buddhism back into India, to recover Buddha Gaya into Buddhist hands, and to re-establish the Sangha in the land of its birth. Fifty years later came the Ambedkar movement, which took advantage of a religious-political situation to bring back millions of Indians into the Buddhist fold. Its future is uncertain, for the Brahmins, who helped to kill the initial Buddhist impulse in India, will not lightly allow millions of their fellow countrymen to change their spiritual allegiance, but the movement back to Buddhism is growing, as is shown by the increasing number of books on the subject published by purely Indian publishers. According to the English Sthavira Sangharakshita, the field that awaits cultivation is enormous and ripe for sowing, but the workers are desperately few.

In Sikkim the movement is well re-established; it is growing, though slowly, in Nepal, largely thanks to the efforts of the Ven. Amritananda, who organized the Congress of the World Fellowship of Buddhists in Katmandu in November, 1956. Ladakh and Bhutan are still virtually closed to foreigners, and the growth of Buddhism therein is problematical. In Tibet there is such powerful resistance to Chinese efforts to purge the nation of its spiritual heritage that the effort seems to have been, for the time being at least, abandoned. More than that one cannot say, but all who have had the privilege of meeting the Dalai Lama, now living in India, will agree that the present holder of that office is a man of great spiritual power, and adored by his people.

In China the flame of Buddhism burns low but is far from being extinguished. A group of Chinese Buddhists from Peking who attended a recent Congress of the World Fellowship of Buddhists were unanimous in stating that they had complete freedom for research, propaganda and to live the Buddhist life, and we heard of new Buddhist institutions of one kind or another being opened in various parts of that enormous country. In South Korea Buddhism is still soundly established.

Japan is rising rapidly in every field, and in friendly and useful contacts with the Western world. Here Buddhism is strong, mostly of the Shin and Zen sects, but with an amazing number of Buddhist groups of every kind springing up spontaneously in various parts of the country. Few would disagree with the suggestion that Japan is the foremost capital of Mahayana Buddhism.

Turning to the Theravada group of countries, these, like Japan, are at present reasonably free to live their Buddhist lives unhindered by the earthy hand of politics. Long may they remain so. If the test of virility is the arising of new ideas and techniques, and the expression of surplus energy in publications, and re-organization within the missions abroad, then Sri Lanka leads the way, although Burma is busy with the reorganization of its Buddhism, particularly in the field of meditation. Thailand, the only Buddhist kingdom, is strongly Buddhist within and, as shown in the Buddhapadipa Temple near London, is capable of sustained missionary effort. Sri Lanka, however, has for long been the most virile. Three of the outstanding movements of the last hundred years have come from this small island; the Maha Bodhi Society, now to be found in a score of Indian cities, the World Fellowship of Buddhists, founded in 1950, and the great Buddhist Encyclopaedia. By these standards Sri Lanka may fairly claim to be the capital of Theravada Buddhism.

Buddhism came to Europe in the form in which, 2000 years earlier, it went further East, that is to say, school by school, each school bringing its own observance and form of organization as the shrine for its essential teaching. In considering the influx of Buddhism into the West—and I am including the USA in this generic term—we must therefore look to the heart of any school and what I call its apparatus. The terms are not synonymous for the one may well be found without the other.

The essential spirit of any school of Buddhism may be gleaned from books, whether its Scriptures or textbooks based upon them, and from talks, whether formal lectures or conversation in class or otherwise. The student, whether college youth or retired businessman, natural recluse or housewife, may have no inclination to look further. There are many in the West—how many we can never know—who, having acquired an understanding of basic principles which appeal to them, set to work to study them, in theory and practice, buying perhaps an occasional new book or borrowing it from a friend or library. They feel no need to join any society and, save for the look of their bookshelves, may remain unknown as 'Buddhists' to all but their closest friends.

They may belong to any school or none. Of the schools of Buddhism the oldest to survive as such is the Theravada, the Doctrine of the Elders, to be found today in Sri Lanka, Burma, Thailand and Cambodia. But the Mahayana, taking this as a general movement, was founded early in the history of Buddhism, and its various schools moved, seriatim, East along the old trade routes into China, Korea and Japan; North into Tibet and Mongolia, and West into North-west India.

In the same way Buddhism became known in the West school by school, first by sporadic translations of isolated scriptures and later by the planned translations of Max Mueller, Rhys Davids and the like who rapidly gave Western scholars a working knowledge of many of their doctrines. But the first organized attempt to make Buddhism known to Western minds as a moral philosophy to be lived, as distinct from being merely studied, was that of the Buddhist Society of Great Britain and Ireland, which was founded in London in November 1907 to prepare the way for Ananda Metteyya, an Englishman who had taken the Robe by that name in Burma and wished to 'proclaim the Dhamma' to his fellow-countrymen. His Buddhism was that of the Theravada. Not until 20 years later, when Dr D. T. Suzuki's *Essays in Zen Buddhism* appeared in London did we know anything, save for an occasional article, about the Zen school of China and Japan, and only in the last 10 years have we begun to learn anything practical about Tibetan Buddhism.

Each of these schools found their specialists, as scholars and practitioners and books have appeared to tell the West more about them. Some were professional scholars; some just wrote of the teaching as it appealed to them; a few, for whom I have dared to coin the phrase 'schollowers', attempt to study and at the same time apply such principles as we glean from the translations of others, though more and more have found the means to study the subject at first hand in the country of their predilection.

Buddhism in the West has the advantage not possessed by the East that wherever the Dhamma is taught the message falls on almost virgin soil, and in a soil that is eager for 'new' ideas of salvation and new meaning for the process of living. Moreover, every self-declared Buddhist is a person so interested in the subject that he has probably left some other system of thought to join it. He is therefore keen in the pursuit of the Way, and in the study of its principles. But his efforts are supported by a powerful body of thinking minds who are 'students of Buddhism', and possibly great authorities in some part of that vast field, without necessarily attempting to apply those principles to daily life. It is a remarkable fact that England led the way in producing for English-speaking people an entire edition of the Pali Canon in English, and this was 30 years at least before any Easterner had it available in his own tongue! The present output of books on Buddhism in English cannot be equalled in India or Sri Lanka, and not yet even in the USA.

Meanwhile, the Buddhist Society, founded in 1924 to succeed the then moribund Buddhist Society of Great Britain and Ireland, has rapidly grown from the position of an obscure little group of Buddhists to a recognized part of the cultural life of London. In its fine new home in Eccleston Square, near Victoria Station, with a Library of 5000 books, a shrine for meditation, and a large Meeting Hall, it offers classes and meetings most nights of the week, and sometimes two in one evening. Its bookstall has grown to the dimensions of a small shop, and its own publications are growing rapidly. All this is evidence of a national movement which, with the aid of 'The Middle Way', which in size and circulation is one of the leading journals in the Buddhist world, is already affecting the leaders of science, psychology and social thought in the West. How long will it be before the three main centres of world Buddhism are Sri Lanka, Japan and England? Some of us now working in the Buddhist field may live to hear the reply.

The Buddhist tide which had flowed West began to flow back into the East, and much of the revival of Buddhism in the East has been Western inspired and often led. Is the time ripe for an attempt to bring all this new strength of purpose and activity into a new collective force of World Buddhism? The attempt is being made. The World Fellowship of Buddhists, the product of the thought and will of one of the greatest Buddhists of our time, Dr G. P. Malalasekera of Ceylon, was born in 1950. Its purpose is to build the potential force contained in the various schools of Buddhism into a mighty spiritual power, with a collective voice to speak and collective means of action, to be used without violence in a violent world towards peace on earth for every man. Is this ideal a foolish dream or is it possible of attainment? The difficulties are considerable and must be faced. The schools use many languages and the Sangha in each is usually the last to learn English. Each country has its Canon, often, as in Soto Zen or Shin, based on the teaching of one man or a single scripture in which at present the other schools show but very little interest.

Again, the forms of ceremony and methods of meditation alike become fixed and traditional. What is worse, they acquire for their followers that 'authority' which the Buddha himself, in the *Kalama Sutta* of the Pali Canon, so strongly condemned. How then are these schools, so various in form, from the moral philosophy of the Theravada or the religious ritual of Tibet to the direct and mentally violent methods of the Zen schools, to be brought together for common action?

If intelligent and well-read members of these various schools, or 'outside' scholar-Buddhists, speaking English and possessed of a strong desire to further the objects of the Fellowship, meet for that purpose, how shall they proceed, and how advise Regional Centres to proceed in pursuance of the common ideal? I suggest that first they must find and briefly formulate a common ground of doctrine on which all schools would agree in general principle. If it is said that such a collection would acquire the status of authoritative dogma, could any set of principles be more dogmatically regarded than the Pali Canon by the average bhikkhu, or the fundamental beliefs of the Nichiren School of Japan in the Lotus Sutra and every word of it?

I submit that if there is to be such a thing as world Buddhism it is time that it were described and its basic nature known. Once formulated, while subject to revision, adaptation and indefinite expansion, this summary should be promulgated by Regional Centres (they having first digested it), to all within reach. And as such principles could be written on a sheet of paper they would be within reach of every school and available for distribution at every Buddhist meeting where the Dhamma is proclaimed. The Buddhist Society's own *Twelve Principles of Buddhism* have been in print in a dozen languages for some 30 years, as the basis of such an enterprise, and have received substantial approval, as set out in my *Via Tokyo* (1948), by authoritative groups of the Sangha in Japan, Burma, Thailand and Sri Lanka.

Then, I suggest, each Regional Centre should begin to broaden the knowledge of those in its area about the existence and differing forms of other Buddhist Schools and practices, working outwards from the principles common to all. Of course each Centre would meet with resistance from the Buddhists of its school, for the ever-lazy will cry, 'Leave us alone—we have all we want', and the Fundamentalists, who exist in every religion, will say, 'We have the Dhamma and that's that'.

Finally, those very few with sufficient breadth of mind to appreciate the range and splendour of the Buddhist field must actively help the headquarters of the Fellowship, wherever situated, to organize succeeding Conferences for the fearless study of Buddhism in all its variety, for objective comparison between its forms, and for methods of offering Buddhist teaching to the modern world of science, psychology and social service in the form most suitable.

But where are these few, and how can they be encouraged to appear? I believe that enough exist to make the attempt at formulating a world Buddhism worth their while, and if strongly encouraged their number may grow. After all, is there any greater gift to mankind than the Dhamma, and if we offer it, why not all of it? And to all?

Search

I seek the One, the final One, but who
    Am I that craves communion?
    Am I but child of all that I have done
    And yet shall do?

I seek, unknowing that I am the sought.
    I search about me for the eyes which see.
    My shouting will is clamorous to be free
    Yet I am nought.

I shrink, and the pale stars grow lighter,
    Fade, and a shadow dies upon the sun.
    Desires die, dissolve, are gone;
    The light grows brighter.

I rise, and earth rejoices at my spending,
    Grow, and the stars are but a garment shed.
    Illusion dies, and lust is dead.
    The self has ending.

15

Why Buddhism?

Future generations may look back on the present era as that of
search, a search for new worlds to conquer, not only in space,
but for discoveries of far more importance, for new values,
new meanings, and above all a new purpose in life. Here am I,
the young say, born into a process of increasing speed to no
worthwhile result; a rat-race for money, power and possessions, and all the prestige and social image that these can buy.
Why should I play?

Neither the search nor the question is new. Always men
have enquired in middle age, having made their fortune, 'Was
all this effort worthwhile?' They feel hollow, and end up with
a breakdown in a psychiatrist's consulting room. And always a
few, while still young, have asked the same question, usually
without reply. Today those few look at their parents and their
parents' friends and ask, as they step on to the moving belt of
'progress', 'What is it for, to prove what, to achieve what?'
They view the long vista of education, job, some fun, a better
job, then marriage and children, more money, middle age,
with possibly some mild distinction and honour and rank. And
they see that the end is always the same, illness, loss of faculty
and death. Does this sound interesting, or exciting or, as more
and more suggest, a frightful bore? The demand grows slowly
within and then bursts out, to parents, teachers and friends, or
in the silence of the night. 'What's it all about? WHAT IS IT
FOR?'

Where do they search? First, in some religion with the
common form of such; in other words for some other means of

salvation than that supplied by Christianity. Second, they examine the growing body of organizations and movements, non-religious and often grossly materialistic, which serve the needs of what is vaguely known as social service, or service to the community. But are they finding what they seek, and if not, why not? Perhaps because they are still seeking without, to a God in heaven, to the 'authority' of some teacher live or dead, or to some new way or path with extravagant claims to be the cure-all for a suffering mankind.

With the help of these they believe that they can change human nature at large and their own in particular. But history has proved them wrong, for no saviour, formula or organization can save mankind or any part of it from the consequence of its own past folly and present state of mind. The purpose of life can only be found in the recorded experience of the great ones of the past, and the testing of those principles by the individual in the intimate details of daily life. This means that the answer lies within, and nowhere else. Here, and only here, in the dismal fog of our private thoughts and feelings, hopes and beliefs, social habits and present set of values, will the truth be found. Not in the mouthings of self-proclaimed Swamis, gurus or the textbooks of untested thought, but within, in the deep thoughts, feelings and intuitions of odd moments of the day or in the quiet hour of prayer or meditation.

Here only will be seen, as a steady glow which grows into the light of enlightenment, the true purpose of Life itself, the answer to the Why and How of our journey to the end of this life and—who knows?—the fresh experience of many a life to come.

Where is the search most strenuous? It would seem in Science, Sociology, Spiritualism and ESP, in Psychology, in Religions new and old, in individual Teachers self-styled of East and West, and in Meditation. In all these groups and movements, which come and go, where does Buddhism stand?

It has firmly arrived in the West and put down roots, but why should the enquirer choose Buddhism?

Three answers may be firmly given. First, because Buddhism includes the whole of the above seven. Second, its history is second to none in the tolerance of its followers in a dozen countries in 2500 years. Judged by history it works. And third, it needs no faith, no apparatus if that term may be used, and applies at all times and in all places and 24 hours a day. There is a fourth answer but it is difficult to say whether it is a reason why Buddhism should be chosen or the reason why many seekers, after giving it a try, move on to something else. This is that in modern parlance Buddhism is a 'do it yourself' way of life, and many enquirers, as some confess, are not really looking for such, but for a Saviour to assume their responsibilities, suffer or forgive their sins, and in brief, so save them. In this Buddhism firmly refuses to help. One more answer may appear later.

Let us see how these areas of search may be grouped under what may be described as planes of consciousness. Science is still of the material plane, being concerned with measurement. But the Buddha was surely the first scientist, in that his approach to all phenomena was objective and empirical. 'Look,' he would say, 'and you will find that all things are inseverable from change. See for yourself that this applies to man, and to all his qualities and principles without exception. There is no immortal or separate self in any of them. And see how every "thing" of every kind is suffused with suffering in one form or another.' Thus these Signs of Being were to be objectively proved, in the sense of scientific examination, by the student for himself. The Buddha's views on the cosmos, on the nature of matter as non-existent, and the ephemeral nature of the ego, were discoveries in the scientific sense, and called for no faith, still less the support of a Teacher's authority.

Sociology is a science of relationships, human relationships, but only between men as citizens. There is here no nobler purpose in life than the physical round of birth, development, decay and death; nothing of the cosmic laws of which man is but the whole in miniature. True, there is a current movement to 'get together', of group effort and co-operative living. But is this progress, or is it psychologically speaking regression into a kind of group soul, wherein the individual is too weak to stand on his own feet and to 'work out his own salvation with diligence', as the Buddha advised?

Spiritualism is on the psychic plane, one above the physical, and so is ESP, the current name for a group of the lower 'powers' in man which should be outgrown as the mind develops. In due course the higher *siddhis* or spiritual powers will develop normally, but only when the person concerned can be trusted not to abuse them or use them to personal ends.

Psychology pertains to the mind and should be a very high science indeed, for it concerns the faculty by which man learns all that may be known about the material world we live in. But it still has in the West a concrete ceiling, and the light of the intuition, the inborn lamp of enlightenment, shines in vain above it. The exception is of course that mighty mind, Carl Jung of Zurich, who perceived the correlations between the spiritual wisdom of the East and his own empirical discoveries in the deeps of his patients' minds. Dr Eric Howe is one of the few with the vision and courage to follow him. But for those in search of a more exalted range of psychology there is the Yogachara school of Mahayana Buddhism and, though the West may never accomplish it, the fascinating use of the mind in Tibetan mystical practices.

Religions are many, though it is usual to speak of the big five. Here the mind and heart, in the East a single dual-meaning word is involved, with higher reaching up into the field of mysticism. The three Theist religions, Judaism, Christianity and Islam have much in common; Hinduism is in a special position with its three-fold trinity of Brahma, Vishnu and Shiva as a threefold aspect of THAT. Buddhism and Taoism find no use for the personal God concept, but have their own description of the Beyond of relativity in the Buddha's words, the 'Unborn, Unoriginated, Unformed' or, abandoning description, 'I shall call it Tao', as Lao-Tse said.

It is here, perhaps that one should place Theosophy, but while it is, as a brief but comprehensive outline of the esoteric Wisdom of the East, the basis and origin of the Teaching which great men in the world's history have given mankind, it is in fact much more. Indeed, in its revealed plan of cosmogenesis itself, and thence of anthropogenesis, the origin and mighty destiny of man, it is the potentially supreme religion, and H. P. Blavatsky's *The Secret Doctrine* may yet be accepted as one of the greatest of religious works available to man.

The search produces solutions, and they are being given the West in increasing quantities by teachers, generally self-declared and prone to sell for much money what they have to give. Their misbehaviour is their own affair, but the rush to sit at their feet must surely demonstrate a craving for salvation by some other, or Other, as it may be regarded. In Buddhism there is no such authority at all, for as the Buddha said, 'Even Buddhas do but point the Way', and he is surely unique in religious history as the only Teacher who told his followers in terms not to accept a doctrine because he gave it them!

Meditation, the immemorial practice of the East, has become a veritable craze in the West, and it is interesting to examine its causes. What do its practitioners seek? The quiet mind, or better, awareness of a deeper, nobler Self within? Or escape from a world the complexities and tensions of which they cannot bear to face? Usually it is only a technique of mind control and in itself gives no knowledge, much less experience of the universal laws of life, nor the awakening of the unappeasable compassion which drives the man of love to the service of his fellow men. And in any event just 'sitting' gets one nowhere. But if the seeker does want meditation there are a dozen proven ways available in the vast field of Buddhism.

With all this variety of solution to the search for a way or purpose in life, why is it suggested that the seeker should choose Buddhism? Let us look further at the reasons already listed.

Careful study will prove that all the solutions suggested by the larger list may be found in the field of Buddhism. Here is true science as applied to the inner mind, the field of spiritual experience. Buddhism today presents a very wide range of philosophy, psychology, religion in its usual sense, morality, social science in a sense as yet unknown in the West, culture and art. It has teachers of all degree and method, from the deeply experienced Lama of Tibet to the Roshi of Japan and the Maha-Thera of the Pali school. And none of these claims authority, nor the power to save a man from his folly nor to lead him to the Goal. And none would sell his teaching or boast of his achievement.

In historical record Buddhism stands unique. There is no word in history of a Buddhist war, waged in the name of the Buddha, nor of persecution for an unacceptable belief, nor even of that intolerance in word and argument which, if it does not reach the fires of Smithfield, mars the religious claims of those who practise it. Judged by the opinions of those who have travelled in Buddhist lands, Buddhism 'works'.

It calls for no faith save that the Buddha did achieve Enlightenment and strove to offer some of its principles to mankind. The rest is experience, the personal rediscovery of the truth put forward. It needs no apparatus, of ritual or prayer, of incense, rosary or shrine. These may be used and are used in the East; they are not of the essence of Buddhism, and are as yet but little adopted in the West. Buddhism is not anchored to a date, and if it were proved tomorrow that the Buddha lived 1000 years earlier or later than the usually accepted date, few would care. It is infinitely adaptable, very different forms of it appearing today in Lhasa and Kyoto and Colombo and London. Yet these are one Buddhism in so many forms. It is essentially a Way, a way of coping with the day's adventures, crises and situations, a Way of reaching Enlightenment for those who truly yearn for it, or for the better helping of mankind for those for whom that noble ideal is sufficient unto the day.

Buddhism, then, is doing Buddhism, a Way, as the Buddha said, from suffering to the end of suffering, from desire to peace. In its higher ranges it aims to destroy the jungle of old thought and fixed belief which limits further action and clouds the mind. With its clear purpose pursued by the total man, cheerfully and with a wide measure of laughter, it has no use for authority of any kind save that of actual experience, and that is to be found in all that we think and feel and do throughout the present day. Slowly the consciousness of the animal is raised at least to that of a thinking mind, however still beset with fear and desire and doubt, and so steadily up the mountain side to illuminated thought, consciousness illumined by the light of the intuition as it slowly wakes with use. And there, if not before, compassion is born, the experience that life is one and inseverable and that, as to helping others, 'there *are* no others'.

All this is discovered whatever one's type, or to use the modern term, conditioning. Do we prefer the moral philosophy of the Theravada, the devotional urge as found in the Shin school of Japan or in the Lotus Sutra, or the ritual practices of Tibet? In the field of psychology, if that is the way preferred, there is a great deal to be learned from existing Buddhist schools, and even in sociology there is a specific Buddhist attitude to the social problems and political argument of the day.

But this is far from all. For the few with trained minds there is available in English what is surely the highest peak of human thought, in a field which is mystical-metaphysics if it can be given a name. In the wide yet in a sense one-pointed theme of the *Prajnaparamita*, 'the Wisdom which has gone Beyond', the Buddhist doctrine of Anatta, no-self, reaches its climax in the doctrine of Emptiness, Sunyata, the Void of all (different) particulars or things. This tremendous range of thought, collating remarkably with the most recent discoveries of physics and astronomy, treats of unlimited space-time which merges in the 'Unborn, Unoriginated, Unformed', which was the Buddha's wording for the Absolute. Yet this indescribable and unnameable Beyond is here and now, in this. 'Look within; thou art Buddha', as we read in *The Voice of the Silence,* and the man and the universe are essentially one.

Here is surely enough! Here is a Way, described in detail to a known end, by the All-Enlightened One, the All-Compassionate One. He will not waste his time who begins to tread it, now. Along its weary way he will suffer, and suffer the more when he learns that all mankind is suffering too, but he will experience the cause of suffering and begin to root it out for himself and all that lives. Is there any more exciting wholetime occupation, which is, with all its tears and darkened wondering, enormous fun!

16

Zen comes West [1]

Buddhism is a Western term for the great body of doctrine, tradition and culture which stems from the enlightenment of Gautama the Buddha. Various schools arose among his followers, including the Theravada, whose canon in Pali began to be written down in the first century BC, and the two schools of the Mahayana, the Madhyamika, associated with the name of Nagarjuna, and the Mind-Only school founded centuries later by Asanga and Vasubandhu.

In due course the teaching of the Buddha in one form or another flowed along the old silk road to China. The Chinese reception to the Message which arrived in the first century AD was cool. Here are monks, the Chinese complained, who do no work to earn their living, have no sons to honour the memory of their parents and are bound by a large number of Rules quite inappropriate to the climate of China.

About 500 AD Bodhidharma, an Indian Buddhist with most unorthodox views and methods of teaching arrived at the Chinese Court and was granted audience with the Emperor. The traditional account of the interview makes it unique in the history of religion.

The Emperor boasted of all he had done to further the cause of Buddhism. He went into detail and asked at the end, 'Now what is my merit?' 'None whatsoever', replied his visitor. The Emperor tried again. 'What is the first principle of Buddhism?' 'Vast Emptiness', replied Bodhidharma, and noth-

[1] This chapter formed the nucleus of *A Western Approach to Zen* (George Allen & Unwin, London, 1972).

ing holy therein'. 'Who, then, now confronts me?' asked the Emperor. 'I have no idea', said Bodhidharma.

The Chinese loved this, though they may not have observed its profundity—and in due course there was born the Ch'an school, which has been described as the Chinese reaction to Indian Buddhism. Further Patriarchs followed Bodhidharma but it was the sixth, Hui-Neng, who turned a new tradition of teaching into an organized school. For 500 years there was a succession of great teachers until, about 1200 AD Ch'an Buddhism arrived in Japan as Zen, where a parallel development took place of the Rinzai and Soto schools.

The essence of Hui-Neng's teaching is clear. It is that of the 'Wisdom that has gone Beyond' (*Prajnaparamita*) of the Madhyamika School as applied directly and without compromise to daily life. Long hours of meditation have their value, but in themselves will no more lead to enlightenment than polishing a tile will turn it into a mirror. There must be the sudden opening of the 'third eye' of Prajna-intuition to see as Hui-neng proclaimed, that 'from the first not a thing is', that 'all distinctions are falsely imagined', that 'in Buddhism there are no two things'. This return to the direct teaching of the Buddha himself was complemented by the later master Huang Po, who taught that 'all sentient beings are nothing but the One Mind, beside which nothing exists.'

Thus in the crucible of direct experience the Ch'an masters fused the teachings of the two great schools of the Mahayana, and applied their wisdom to work in the fields, the market and the home.

Stories about these masters were collected and handed down, as also specimens of the mondo or rapid question/answer by which the master would attempt to help the pupil break out of the fetters of his thinking. But whereas the early masters taught their pupils face to face according to their need, later masters began to rely on the koan, of which the first on record is that of Hui-Neng himself, who persuaded the robber pursuing him to sit in silence for a while, after which he asked him, 'When you are thinking neither of good nor evil, what is at that moment your original face (or Essence of Mind)? 'These enigmatic sayings or questions, without obvious sense, are used to break the mould of thought and to release the mind 'to abide nowhere'.

Hundreds of koans were in time produced, such as 'What is the sound of one hand clapping?', and even classified, and for the last 1200 years the training in Rinzai Zen Buddhism has been based upon them. But whereas this is evidence that the system works for a Japanese monk in a monastery, it is poor evidence that it would be right for a Western mind in daily life. In my experience the koan system should not be used in the absence of a qualified teacher, for it involves the production of increasing pressure in the mind of the pupil who is driven, as it were, down a blind alley with a brick wall at the end of it. If a competent master is watching the final stages, ready, as it is said, to help the chicken break out of the egg and, equally important, ready to approve the resulting 'experience' and to help with the long process of 'maturing' it, the method may succeed for the few. But in the absence of such a master the pressure may actually break the mind concerned and produce not enlightenment but insanity.

Then what is left for Europe? Zen training in Japan involves long days and years of deep meditation, whether on the given koan or, as in Soto Zen, just 'sitting' and this assumes a monastic life and almost unlimited time. Nowadays a few go to Japan from the West, learn Japanese and submit themselves to the training, but so far none have returned to Europe with approved enlightenment. Conversely, Rinzai masters have visited Europe, occasionally for months on end, and accepted pupils for the duration of the visit. These visits have not been a success if only because the time available was quite inadequate. I therefore take the view, expressed these last 10 years, that the hundreds of Western Buddhists genuinely interested in Zen Buddhism must find an alternative to the traditional training of Japan. Here are four reasons for this grave decision:

1. It is unreasonable to expect Europeans of today to adopt a

system of spiritual training formulated for the Chinese in 700 AD.

2. If it *were* right for Europe, it would need a large body of qualified Japanese teachers, between them speaking many languages and prepared to give long years to training those students who wished to become their pupils. Conversely, the training would be confined to the few Westerners with the time and money for a long visit to Japan.

3. The faculty by which, in Buddhist terms, the West is working out its *dharma* is the intellect, a superb instrument for the acquisition of truth in the field of duality. In my view it cannot be by-passed or ignored. It must be developed and used to the full before the Western consciousness can, by developing the intuition, transcend its inherent limitations and achieve a direct vision of Reality. Only by reaching the end of thought shall we break through to the beyond of thought, which is Prajna-intuition, the 'third eye' with which alone we shall perceive and know that we already are enlightened.

4. We in the West are householders, and monastic life is no longer normal save for the few. We have a part to play in the total life of the community. While using meditation as a planned part of the daily life we must find an approach to Zen awareness which uses the day's adventure to that end.

Much of the intellectual background of Zen Buddhism is now available in English. Thanks to the work of Dr Edward Conze, we have much of 'the Wisdom that has gone Beyond', and we have some 20 books of the scriptures of Zen Buddhism, its meaning and practice, from the late Dr D. T. Suzuki, who gave his life to making known as much as words may tell us of this, perhaps the most truly Buddhist school of Buddhism. But it is not enough to arouse interest and provide the intellectual background. There must be a definite method of self-training aimed at a break-through to the 'Unborn, Unoriginated, Unformed'. What is it to be? That is the problem, and it is not new. I drew attention to it in 1960 in a book called

Zen Comes West, and I have so far heard no answer other than my own.

It involves a long course of mind-training, parallel with those of the Theravada and the various traditions of Tibet. It needs some preliminary mind development acquired in this life or in lives gone by; the will-power necessary to carry through any training once begun, however strange and seemingly difficult; and commonsense in application.

But here is a crisis, not to be lightly ignored. As Hui-Neng and his successors point out, with all the force at their command, it is impossible to enlighten the mind, for the mind, as an inseverable part of All-Mind or Buddha-Mind, is already enlightened. As Hui-Neng, with a thunder voice proclaimed, 'From the first not a thing is,' and this is the heart of the *Prajnaparamita* philosophy which is the highest that Buddhism or any other philosophy-religion has attained. Or, in the words of Huang Po again, 'All sentient beings are nothing but the One Mind, besides which nothing exists'. It seems to follow that, viewed on its own plane, the enormous complex of thought, feeling, will and desire that we call mind can never *become* the Buddha-Mind, for it is attachment to its product, thought, which alone prevents us seeing that we are in essence already Buddha-Mind, which includes both Nirvana and Samsara, the Absolute of Non-duality and the relativity of daily life. To work on this mind is therefore more than unnecessary, worse than useless; it is pernicious, in that it may but pander to a subtly inflated ego.

How, then, shall we dare to do this very thing, to work on the present mind with a view to seeing that we are, and have been all the time, enlightened? How shall we dare to train this individual mind which, on the plane of Buddha-Mind, does not even exist? I answer boldly, because the difference between mind and Buddha-Mind is, like all distinctions, in the words of Hui-Neng, 'falsely imagined'. We are mind as much as we are Buddha-Mind, and the Course which I suggest destroys this false antithesis, as equally that of self and Self, of the flame and the Light. Surely the whole man climbs to the summit, 'muddy boots and all', taking all things with him, good and evil, truth and lies, to re-become the Essence of Mind which never ceased to be his own divinity.

When, therefore, the masters of Zen appeal to us 'to drop it', meaning mind and all to do with it, or emphasize that 'all duality is falsely imagined', surely we have here such a false antithesis? Should we not use the mind we have and largely are, to achieve reunion with its source? But I agree that the distinction must be *seen* to be false, not merely with a thought, however illumined, but with the light of intuition as immediate, direct awareness, a break-through to Reality.

But HOW? How does the average, dedicated Western seeker after Life and its own high purpose begin to lift his consciousness to the plane where all these splendid sayings are true? The Buddha gave an answer, that of the Noble Eightfold Path, which includes right purpose largely bereft of selfishness, right action in the world of men, and then right training of the mind to the level of Samadhi, the sweet calm of perfect mind-control. Did all the Zen masters find a by-pass round this clearly defined, hard way? Or are they speaking from the level of achieved attainment when, illusion shed, they see from the deeps of a Buddha-Mind that they have never ceased to be? If so, how did they get there?

Surely there must be analysis before synthesis, examination of the illusion we must learn to see as such, awareness of infinite difference before a realization that the Many never cease to be One.

Even if the purpose of Zen training is to see that there is nothing to attain, whence this 'seeing', save by examination, with the highest mind we can command, of the nature of Samsara, which we are told we shall one day know to be Nirvana in its earthly guise? And this involves the training and the right use of the mind.

I suggest that what is needed by the Western student, and was once in some form used by all who now speak from the plane of Prajna-intuition, is a flight of steps up which we *gradually* climb the '100-foot pole', from the top of which we jump, with the existential leap, into *sudden* Zen awareness.

The steps here suggested, all of which are within the ambit of the seventh and eighth of the Eightfold Path, have the merit of being reasonable, suited to the Western mind and temperament, safe in the absence of a qualified teacher for much at least of the climb, and above all they work! Slowly, steadily, safely, we raise consciousness until, progressively illumined by the growing light of enlightenment, we are ready for the first 'peeps' of the new awareness, and meanwhile serve with humble, dedicated heart the needs of all mankind.

This is no place to set out the Course of long self-training which, from raw experience in my own life and in the Zen Class of the Buddhist Society, I offer to the Western seeker after Zen.

I can but summarize the notes included for each Phase which, over the period of months allocated, are expanded, discussed and used as the basis for consistent meditation.

PHASE ONE. 'UNTHINK'

Before thought can be transcended we must examine the nature of thought, the thought process and the extent to which our minds are now conditioned by past thinking, present thought-habits and habitual reaction to stimulus.

Before we can build 'the 100-foot tower' from which we take 'an existential leap' into the enlightenment-experience we must largely clear the foundations of outworn thought and now unneeded thinking.

Only then shall we be able to practise genuine thought-control, the quieting down of the waves of thought, and reach 'the still centre of the turning world', the Buddha-Mind within.

First, then, let us look at our present general and particular conditioning, and make some attempt at 'de-conditioning', to break our bondage and clear up the resulting mess.

At the close of each Phase we ask ourselves searching questions. Here we ask, 'How much am I still bound to particular views on religion, politics, social problems? Can I honestly see the other man's point of view on anything in issue, anything at all? And finally, can I visualize, however dimly, a Truth which is above and beyond both of any pair of opposites, which *was* before the difference was born?'

PHASE TWO. 'STOP THINKING'

Having faced the mind's conditioning and begun to detach it from outworn thoughts and undesirable thought-habits we must go further.

We shall not in fact stop thinking for there is no need, but we must learn to decide what we think, and when and why, and to turn off the tap when finished. The same will apply to controlling our reactions to outside stimulus or to invading thoughts from within.

The all-but-impossible ideal is to 'let the mind abide nowhere' or, in the words of the Heart Sutra, to 'dwell without thought-coverings.' We are yet far from it. Let us move just that much nearer.

After months of this we shall ask ourselves questions, such as, 'Can I now for minutes on end stop all reaction to outside events or objects, not in deep meditation but as I move around? Can I cease at will from 'mental chattering'? In particular, can I stop approving or disapproving of what others do or say? Can I really mind my own business? Have I the moral strength to refuse to form an opinion about happenings around me or at large? Can I frankly change an opinion once formed?'

Up to this point we are pupils back at school, with a list of books for study, loose-leaf notebooks and a compulsory period each day for study and/or meditation as found needful. The theme being used at the time is held at the back of the mind all day, to come forward into consciousness at every moment when the mind is free to work on it. The pupil is not yet concerned with Zen experience or anything to do with 'Zen'.

CONCENTRATION AND MEDITATION

The clear distinction between these two employments of the mind should be thoroughly understood. Western Buddhists today are much concerned with meditation, but the practice is entangled with too much technical jargon. Meditation is not natural to the mind and should if practised remain as simple as possible. Surely it is sufficient to learn to concentrate and then, when opportunity permits, to turn a search-light into the mind in search of Buddha-Mind. Such at least is the belief of many.

PHASE THREE. 'RETHINK'

Now for the first time the mind is lifted as high as may be into the realm of intuitive awareness. What is Zen? Alas, 'the Tao (or Zen or Truth) that can be named (described) is not the eternal Tao' (or Zen or Truth). Zen is not a thing, not an idea nor yet a noble ideal. Nor can it be attained for we live already in its abiding place, Pure-Mind.

One day we shall find that all thought stands in the way of our enlightenment. Not yet. We must now deliberately use great thought to raise consciousness to the threshold of a new faculty, the intuition. This will increasingly illumine thinking until the first brief moments come of direct immediate vision of things as they are, beyond duality of thought or feeling. These great thought-forces must be invited, deeply studied and allowed to remould the total man. There will be conflict, for the price of victory is the death of self.

Here is the heart of the system of self-training which I have used for 50 years and humbly advocate. Let but one of these vast 'Thought-forces' enter the mind *at its own level*, or as near as may be, and the total man is re-created. This is a claim which argument cannot affect; it will be found to be true or not. There is here no fear of an uncontrolled irruption from the unconscious; these thoughts are welcome guests, flames of the Light, as a light switched on to dispel the deep gloom of illusion. To use them is to remove all fear of the manifold forms of pseudo-Zen, the snatching of unlawful moments of a false awareness by selfish pressure to attain. These trance conditions and forced glimpses of the psychic plane are as different from the 'no-moment' of true Satori as pewter from pure gold, deceiving no one but the fool who waits to be deceived. There are no short cuts to enlightenment.

These cosmic principles are difficult to imprison in a phrase, for though each was once a shrine for a vast experience, the words have largely lost their meaning and become the debased coinage of third-rate literature. 'Life is One' is a fair example, tremendous in its implications, from the brotherhood of man to the fact that there is no death, save of an outworn form. 'From the first not a thing is' said Hui-Neng. Can our present mind conceive, and use, such pure idealism? It can try. That Prajna, Wisdom, and Karuna, Compassion, are one inseverable unity is, according to Dr Suzuki, the basis of Mahayana. Here the Arhat and the Bodhisattva doctrines are seen to be indivisible, and the Bodhisattva doctrine is, I believe, fast gaining ground in the field of Western thought. Again, Karma is much more than the drear equation of cause-effect; it is rather a sweeping vision of the Universe as total Harmony, which broken, the breaker first and then all manifestation must restore. Thus Karma is seen as the regulator of the Unborn/born relation and of the least part of it. And finally, in this choice from dozens such, 'It's all right' or, as a Zen master put it, 'the snowflakes fall, each in its proper place'. Or as the American poet, Thoreau, put it, 'I know that the enterprise is worthy. I know that things work well. I have heard no bad news'.

As these forces surge and thunder through the mind, smashing the barriers of outworn thought, dissolving the ego, washing away distinctions, limitations and choices grimly held, consciousness is raised just that much nearer to the level of its own true home, 'the Essence of Mind' which is, as Hui-Neng put it, 'intrinsically pure'. Here is the field of what I call Illumined Thought, great thinking lit with increasing certainty as the light of the intuition proves or disproves the concepts dwelling in the mind.

Such a condition is visible to all, for all 'great' minds, so-called by their fellows, are expanded and illumined minds, illumined, one would say with the Buddha-light of Prajna-intuition, the 'third eye' opened to see things as they are. Many such minds are clearly often more than so illumined; they have achieved some measure of Satori. Many of the finest philosophers, astronomers, scientists, poets, statesmen, ecclesiastics, men of commerce and of war, have spoken of experience which can be fairly so described. And there is here no limiting claim for Buddhist influence. It is of interest that several of the few already known to us whose 'break-through', has the marks of authenticity had never heard of Buddhism, still less of Zen.

Meanwhile the student, secure in illumined thought, looks for a bridge from duality to Non-duality, from the unreal to the Real. In truth there is none and can be none, yet the bridge is crossed, the journey made, and safely now. Knowledge, become Wisdom, flowers in compassion. Possessed of sound character, moved with true motive, safe from the 'ballooning' of the ego and the seduction of short-cuts the climber climbs with skilful mountaineering. Each 'peep' of Reality is a solid gain. There is *gradual* progress of the total man to *sudden* bright experience. In due course, 'when the pupil is ready the master appears'. We shall have earned him.

PHASE FOUR. 'BEYOND THOUGHT'
As the ceiling of Samsara, the dual world of unreality, is pierced with the sword of Prajna-intuition, allowing 'peeps'

145

K

of a wider state of consciousness, we reach the true beginning of Zen training. Each experience is incommunicable in words but each has the common factor that self has disappeared. These are 'moments of awareness', not of my awareness of any thing which was not there before. Here subject/object, past, present and future, you and I no longer exist in separation. We now see everything as it is, and all things as inseverable parts of the same Fullness/Emptiness. This is the true beginning of Zen training which Dr Suzuki called 'a moral training based on the experience of Satori'. Let us walk on!

Part Four

ON DOING BUDDHISM

17

On Doing Buddhism

This chapter might have been called 'A Study in Karma and Right Action', but that would be doctrine, and I am here totally concerned with Action. The field is unlimited and the theme is worthy of a book. Here at the most are but 15 'chapter headings' for that almost unlimited volume.

1. ALL IS ACTION

From the moment the 'Unborn' is born onto the field of manifestation, until this 'unrolling of the worlds', as it is called in the Pali Canon, becomes 'the rolling up of the worlds', ALL IS ACTION. Nothing *is* save a ceaseless process of 'coming to be, coming to be' followed by 'ceasing to be, ceasing to be'. Life is motion and all is alive. Forms are born, grow, grow old and wear out—Life goes on, Life, the creative/destructive Force of manifestation whether known as Buddha-Mind, the Dharma-kaya or Almighty God. Nirvana is awareness of the Void of separate forms; Samsara is the changing world of forms. Each is a mode of the other; 'Form is emptiness and the very emptiness is form', says the Heart Sutra. Wisdom *is* action. As Dr Suzuki wrote, 'Prajna (Wisdom) is activity itself'. Thus although Samsara is one vast bubble of *maya*, illusion, we live and grow and attain enlightenment within this illusion, suffering its inevitable tension of duality and involved in its unceasing action, whether its form be action, re-action or no action.

2. 'BUDDHISM IS A WAY OF DOING BUDDHISM'

Buddhism is a way, a way of Right Action, 'right' meaning perfect. Indeed, as I wrote elsewhere, 'A sufficient philosophy of life may be devised about the right doing of the job, whatever it may be, in hand. For we are all of us, in one way or another, in action 24 hours a day, and as we are doing something all the time it is reasonable to learn to do it rightly'. (From *The Way of Action*). This, as we soon find out, involves deliberate self-training, carried out at every moment and in every place. As Dr Suzuki wrote in the *Eastern Buddhist* (Vol. I, p. 358), 'We now come to the most characteristic feature of Zen Buddhism. In fact the truth of Zen is the truth of life, and life means to live, to move, to act and not merely to reflect'.

3. ACTION INVOLVES ALL TYPES OF MIND

All minds are acting at all times and in every situation. We cannot 'opt out', nor escape from the stream of life of which we are an undivided part. All four of Carl Jung's famous diagram of types are equally involved; the intellectual and the feeling types, the intuitive and the sensuous. So are the introvert and the extravert, though they act in very different, complementary ways. In the field of religion we have in Hinduism the Jnana, Bhakti and Karma Yogin, the sage of enormous intellect, the saint of pure devotion and love, and the man of action, respectively. In this analysis it seems that the Anglo-Saxon races are mainly Karma yogins, for in any situation they ask, 'What do I *do*?' and Buddhism supplies the answer out of the ultimate law, Karma.

But to the Buddhist the most important division of type is that between the Arhat and the Bodhisattva. The former is concerned with his own mind, its control, purification, expansion and enlightenment. He will then, he believes, be in a position to help his neighbour and all mankind. The Bodhisattva is unconcerned with his own enlightenment; his vast compassion drives him to the service of all forms of life; assisting each with his unending 'skilful means', 'until the last blade of grass has entered into enlightenment'. Of course, no man is totally either, and of course the two are complementary in that the ideal man is both. But it should be of interest to the student, and helpful, to study where he stands, in the psychological analysis of Jung, the triple division of Raj Yoga and the visible duality of purpose in the Arhat and Bodhisattva ideal.

4. ACTION AND THE ACTOR

We must further examine the nature of the actor, of whatever type, of his action and the relation between them, and of 'agenda', a word meaning things meet to be done, whether the list be a plan for life or a shopping list. If these things should be done let them be done; if not, leave them undone.

It is often asked, usually by the artistic type, 'Why all this dreary self-analysis? Why not act spontaneously?' There are two main answers. First, that we can't. We are so conditioned by past action and thought in adult life, before that by birth, education and environment in childhood, and before that by the net resultant of long lives of previous growth, that we cannot now act quite spontaneously. The second answer is that if the questioner really can do so, as distinct from acting on impulse arising from that conditioning, he would be a very advanced man indeed and not asking the question!

5. HOW FREE ARE WE TO ACT AS WILLED?

The answer for most of us is, very little. The bonds of past conditioning are far more powerful than we realize, and that which was knotted years and lives ago cannot be lightly loosed. The operative law is Karma, the ultimate law of the universe. I visualise the coming forth of THAT, the Unborn, as producing when manifest a total and inviolate harmony in all its parts, in its central Life-force and its mode of change. Man breaks that harmony, a hundred times a day, and suffers, in that he who breaks must mend. Who else, if there be justice anywhere? On the ceaseless round of 'coming to be, coming to be' each human being produces a stream of causes, on all planes of consciousness, and is responsible for every one of them. Each such unit is the product of its own past choosing, conditioned by its own past action, in thought and in deed, and in the illusion of time will bear (suffer) the perpetually modified results. I agree with Talbot Mundy in *Black Light*, 'Each deed done is a promissory note to meet its consequences'. Of course, the implications of this concept shake the mind to its foundations, but that does not invalidate the Law, the living Law, by which we live, in which we move, which truthfully, in utter fact, we are.

This is not merely my own belief, nor that of Buddhism. Arnold Toynbee, the distinguished historian, wrote recently, 'Every generation, and every individual, inherits the burden of karma, the consequences of earlier action. We have it in our power to mitigate our inherited karma or to aggravate it, but we cannot jump clear of it, and we ignore it at our peril'.

If this be true, or a working hypothesis of truth, we cannot avoid the consequences, 'good' or 'bad' as we may label them, of any act. Not in a vihara, in pleasure, in 'not thinking about it', in meditation or in the market place. Not, as the *Dhammapada* puts it, 'in the sky nor in the sea nor in a cave in the mountains can a man escape his evil deeds'. Or, for that matter, his good ones. Nor in death, for the dissolution of the outer envelope of man, the body, does not release him from the operation of the Law. The 'bundle of characteristics' which makes up the 'self' in any life is re-assembled for the next rebirth, in a fresh set of outer garments, and takes the consequences of the past life's virtue and folly.

The deeper understanding of the Law destroys, I submit, any further talk of chance, or 'unalterable Fate' or even of coincidence. In Buddhism there is only an inconceivable precision of cause–effect, operating on all planes, mental, psychic and physical. Only the Self, the Buddha-Mind, is above its sway, on its own plane. The Law is just, and we are well advised to take heed of our least action, for the act itself demands and will exact an utterly right payment.

6. THE ACTOR AND HIS PRINCIPLES

Man is twofold, as in the Pali Canon ('Self is the lord of self. What other lord should there be?'). Or threefold, as in the practical and helpful 'body, soul and Spirit' of St Paul, the personality at the base with its animal instincts and low desire, the Buddha-Mind at the top and, in between, call it what you will, the ever-reborn entity which is not eternal but coheres as an entity until, in our growing wisdom, we dissolve it. Or sevenfold, in Indian philosophy, which distinguishes the mind and the intuition, and below, the psychic and physical planes. In any event the total man is many principled, from Atman, one with the Dharma-kaya, the Unborn, down to *rupa*, the final envelope of clay. On each and every plane consciousness, backed by the growing will, functions and produces effects, either helping to the total Purpose of the Unborn, or fighting it. In the ideal man there is perfect alignment from top to bottom, a total, self-perfected man.

7. ALL ACTION IS IN THE MIND

Each act is born in the mind, which is where we begin to 'do Buddhism'. Both higher and lower mind create thoughts, which are, as such, 'things', with varying shape, duration and quality. Each is a form of the one Life-force of the universe, and therefore bears results. It follows that we should indeed be 'mindful and self-possessed', as the Pali Canon advises, for the *Dhammapada* is right in declaring, in Verse I, that 'all that we are is the result of what we have thought'! Indeed, we *are* our thoughts, good, bad, and indifferent, in a complex mass of conflicting impulses, desires, and principles, bound into a semblance of unity with hopes and fears and loves and hates and a vast fog of illusion. The final section of the Buddha's Noble Eightfold Path is right, therefore, in calling for self-discipline to produce the right mindfulness, so that we only think and feel what leads to compassion and the heart's delight, to a greater degree of enlightenment.

We can only at any time affect our conscious life; psychology has proved how much more is unconscious, which must, that it may be brought under control, be rescued from that condition. This is one of the purposes of meditation, to release the forces of the unconscious into consciousness, and thence to control. Only thus will the great mass of our conditioning be slowly dissolved, and the ideal state of mind be that much nearer, 'to awaken the mind to abide nowhere'. Here is the perfect thought-control, where no fresh karma is made, or good or bad, for the mind has ceased to create it. Thereafter a thought will be created and used, precisely and only as needed; meanwhile it is enough to say, 'I follow my karma as it moves', while taking care to make no more. Concentrating on the next act to be done, perfectly, there is full attention to causes and indifference to effects. Thus will the cause in time be causeless, for self, breeder of all mistakes and foolish action, the spanner in the works of our endeavour, will, like a fire that dies for want of fuel, slowly disappear.

8. ACTION 'RIGHT' AND 'WRONG'

How shall we know the difference? What is good and what is evil? The answer lies in motive, which is not the same thing as purpose or intent. The purpose of meditating, for example, may be to gain mind-control. The motive for this may be the better to serve mankind, but it may also be to get the better of a business rival, or to put oneself forward as a great teacher. Indeed, 'there's nothing good or bad but thinking makes it so', and the test is the presence of self. Are we flowing *with* the cosmic tide in all we think and do, or against it? Are we working for self or for the whole? Moving inwards towards the centre or outwards towards difference, distinction and the self's aggrandisement?

It has been said that the perfect act has no result, for there is no one there to receive it. There was right action, indifferent to result. As Tennyson wrote in *Oenone*,

> 'Self-reverence, self-knowledge, self-control,
> These three alone lead life to sovereign power.

Yet not for power (power of herself
Would come uncalled for), but to live by law
Acting the law we live without fear;
And because right is right, to follow right
Were wisdom in the scorn of consequence'.

And the law we live by is the Law of Karma, of cosmic harmony, of cause–effect in this life and all others, past and yet to come.

9. RIGHT ACTION IS ON A MIDDLE WAY

The least variance from a balanced middle way is a move toward one extreme, and all extremes are bad. Yet we are not concerned with compromise, a little of this and a little of that, but with a raised awareness to the point when both extremes are seen as modes or aspects of each other. We think of a coin with its 'heads' and 'tails'. They are modes of the coin. We think of heat and cold; they are the absence of each other. We speak of Spirit and matter; they are one. The Arhat and the Bodhisattva, already mentioned, do not walk on either side of a middle way; both are in the centre, but note, if you are prepared for the final and only language of spiritual truth, paradox, that the Middle Way by definition has no middle. Tread it.

10. THE PRICE PAID FOR RIGHT ACTION

Nothing in life is free. The price of right action is self, the foolish belief that 'I' am different from, and eternally different from 'you', when in truth we are but different forms, for ever changing, of the Life-force of the Ultimate. The awareness of this truth brings suffering, and the appearance of sacrifice. But as the Lama said in Talbot Mundy's *Om*, 'There is no such thing as sacrifice; there is only opportunity to serve'.

The test becomes acute under the heading of Right Livelihood. Is your job compatible with Buddhist principles? If not, have you the enormous courage to leave it, quite possibly for something less well paid? Many are doing so. All honour to them for 'doing Buddhism'.

And we must learn to withdraw at least the worst of our projections, cease to blame others for all that we do not like, learn to be 'nothing special', as the Zen men say, to be vulnerable to all 'the slings and arrows of outrageous fortune', and take things as they come. This itself is a noble form of right action.

11. THE DAY'S AGENDA

The day's agenda is a list of things to be (rightly) done. As such, each item is of the same importance. Dharma, the complex term for the Buddha's teaching, his norm, or Law, is for each of us at any moment our duty—that unpopular word —which lies in that portion of Dharma which is our life's and the moment's karma. I have often said that my personal God is made of paper, being a list of the things to be done that day, in the right order, in the best place and at the right time. And with the right motive, and the power to forget them as soon as rightly done. The list may include planning for the future, or deliberate rest, or study, or meditation, or shopping, or coping with your own and with others' problems, crises, awkward situations.

To do it because it is the next thing to be done produces self-control, of all one's instruments and faculties, and this produces control of the situation. It deflates the ego, helps to produce that 'constant and unwavering steadiness of heart upon the arrival of every event, whether favourable or unfavourable', as advised by the *Bhagavad Gita*. It brings the only freedom, a readiness to be a small but living cog in the universal process, neither interfering with others ('There is danger in another's duty'), nor omitting a single chance to help ('Inaction in a deed of mercy is an action in a deadly sin'). One sees that Life is indeed one, and all its forms completely interrelated.

12. NON-ACTION AS RIGHT ACTION

No-action can be immensely powerful, and Non-action, the ideal of the *Tao-Te-Ching* is best of all. 'Be humble and you will remain entire' is a quotation from it, and the operative word is remain. Be chary of all action lest it be unwise, unneeded, fraught with self, but if you act the immediate purpose may be small indeed. 'The sage never attempts great things, and thus he can achieve what is great'. A bricklayer can only lay one brick. Let us take the next step, for the rest will follow.

13. WALK ON!

The process of coming-to-be, ceasing-to-be, knows no pause; still less does it ever stop. The past accumulation of karma exerts unceasing pressure on the present, and the demands of the moment must be met here and now. For me the pilgrim's progress is a soldier's march, 'left-right, left-right, left-right', which never hesitates whatever karma stands in the way. Problems, crises may appear ahead. Walk on! 'Left-right, left-right'. If you come to a brick wall, go through it; to a precipice, go over it, but don't stop!

Each day we face a hundred situations, large and small, from an absent milk bottle on the doorstep to being given the sack, or a legacy, or hearing of a dear one's death. In my Zen class we consider the right reaction to such events. Each situation, we say, has seven ingredients, of which the first is that 'It isn't there!' All is Void, a Void of all separate things, including this situation, for all Samsara is Mahamaya, the great illusion, only the 'Be-ness' of the Unborn, Unoriginated Absolute being true. Second, we remind ourselves that anyhow it is our karma, and it is useless to project the blame on anyone else; and third, as part of the living Law of Karma, it is *all Right*. Members of the class dislike all three suggestions but they happen to be true. There is, alas, no time here for the other four.

14. THE TAKE-OVER

My task grows harder, for this is a purely personal experience, though known to many, and difficult to describe. There is indeed what Edwin Arnold called in *The Light of Asia,* 'Before beginning and without end . . . a Power divine which moves to good. Only its laws endure'. Let us call it the Buddha-Mind, which Huang Po calls 'the One Mind beside which nothing exists'. The feeling, all agree, is a paradoxical blend of receiving instruction while being in entire control of oneself and the situation. Truly, 'there is a divinity doth shape our ends, rough hew them as we will', and the wise man, Buddhist though he claims to be, should look again at the heart of Christianity: 'Thy will be done'. For the Will to which we kneel is no less than the Buddha-Mind within ('Look within: thou *art* Buddha'). There is nothing indeed which is not divine, and we must exercise what Gerald Gould perfectly describes, 'this careless trust in the divine occasion of our dust'. Under this inspiration, or with this guidance, one *becomes* the act, and there is no actor left to flaunt his motive nor await his earned reward. And no such act is wasted. May I quote from Browning's *Abt Vogler*?

> There shall never be one lost good. What was, shall live as before.
> The evil is null, is nought, is silence implying sound;
> What was good shall be good with, for evil, so much good more.
> On the earth the broken arcs; in the heaven the perfect round.
> All we have willed or hoped or dreamed of good shall exist,
> Not the semblance but its self; no beauty nor good nor power
> Whose voice has gone forth, but each survives for the melodist
> When eternity affirms the conception of an hour.

15. THE LIFT TO NON-ACTION

Description becomes increasingly difficult. It is all too easy to discuss the concepts of No-thought and Purposelessness; to attain the least awareness of their meaning is far different. But they shine as an ideal. How lovely to follow R. H. Blyth's advice, and practise 'the infinite way of doing finite things'. We shall, but perhaps not yet. But with persistent study, and meditation in one form or another, and the will to apply our understanding to every moment of the day, we may begin to see action, Right action, as itself both way and goal. When the whole man is harnessed to this end, when study has lifted habitual thought to the level of illumined thought, as I have called it, there will be 'peeps' of intuitive awareness of the thing as it is, its suchness or 'isness', and this is the same for every form of the one indivisible Life.

And so to doing Buddhism, and the opening suggestion that 'Buddhism is doing Buddhism'. It is the way of spiritual crafts-manship, of a million things well done. It brings satisfaction, the meaning of which is so interesting, 'doing enough'. When we have done enough in relation to any thing to be done we have done enough. We may rest if we wish, but there is always another item on the list, and will be 'until the last blade of grass has entered enlightenment'. Let us forget reward or recognition or even enlightenment. And why? Because we shall be too busy to give them heed.

But doing Buddhism needs guts, enormous guts, increas-ingly applied. It calls, I suggest, for at least five qualities, some of them for some of us new.

(1) A clear sense of purpose, and the strength of will to maintain it. (2) Nobility of thought, which strives to under-stand the nature and purpose of THAT, which gave birth to the field of illusion which we call Samsara. (3) Nobility of character involving a high sense of morality in a world which has largely forgotten the meaning of the term. (4) Increasing dominion over self, by letting it peacefully die for want of nourishment. (5) For some the most important of all, an increasing love of all beings until one finds as a fact that there

are no others, to hate or love. All these are slowly developed in the whole-time, utterly fascinating work of doing Buddhism, and one at least who strives has found it to be quite enormous fun!

18

Buddhism in Daily Life

Buddhism, then, is a way of life, from first to last a matter of experience. For the Way is a way to the supreme experience by which Gautama, the ˙man, became Buddha, the Fully Awakened One. Buddhism, therefore, though including a set of doctrines alleged to be the Buddha's Teaching must, if it is to be true to its genesis, be at the same time a matter of doctrine applied. The Buddha's call was to move from the static to the dynamic, to eschew all futile argument on the 'Indetermin-ates', such as the nature of the First Cause or of the Self and to move and keep on moving towards Enlightenment. For these questions can never *ex hypothesi* be usefully answered. The First Cause is necessarily beyond, because prior to, causation, and that which is out of manifestation is beyond the reach of words. Buddhism, then, has no use for belief, save in the sense that 'a man believes a doctrine when he behaves as if it were true'. Nor has it any place for faith, save in the reasonable description by a guide of a Path and its Goal: 'Thus have I found', said that Guide, 'and this is the Way to that discovery. I tell you the steps on the Way, its dangers and difficulties, the fierce resistance offered by the self, the lures to beguile you into some other way which leads still deeper into the mire of suffering'. Meanwhile, that the Way is worthy, as Mrs Rhys Davids would have said, may be proved at every stage. For treading it there are two rules and only two: Begin, and walk on. Once the first step is taken—and where else than here and now?—each further stage will reveal a wider range of view, an air more pure to breathe, more light from the Indivisible as the clouds of our present illusion and desire are, not so much dispersed, as quietly plodded through.

The beginning and end of the Dhamma, then, is experience, the Buddha's supreme experience under the Bo-Tree, and yours and mine. All doctrines constellate about it. The Signs of Being are characteristics of the world about us, which we ourselves created and in our reaction to which we gain the experience by which we climb. Experience in action is Karma, and though its implications are frightening, with an utter absence hereafter of chance and luck and coincidence, we must be brave and walk with courage in a world wherein each littlest action is the fruit of a million causes, and our every thought and act the father of a million effects. If our responsibility grows each hour for all that we think and feel and do, let us live accordingly, with newly controlled, self-conscious, thoughtful lives. And the right use of Karma is to apply it to the Four Noble Truths. Is not all in some sense suffering? Is not its cause the illusion of self and the cries of self for self in the darkness of illusion? How, then, shall we remove the cause of the cause, the desire which makes us do the acts which cause the suffering? The answer is, by treading a Path, ever more fully revealed as it mounts the hillside by a way made visible, if not yet easy, by the feet of those in front of us, to a summit which we shall not 'know' until we reach it. Yet sometimes, when the night is at its darkest hour, we experience, as lightning in the mind, a direct and blinding glimpse of that Light which will, when we have made it so, be the common light of day.

Buddhism, then, is the process of learning by experience to approach, by a gradual or a 'sudden' path, the supreme experience of the All-Enlightened One. The knowledge of the scholar will prepare the mind; the debates of the intellect may clear the way of intellectual fog; but just as we begin to drive a car when it first moves under our wondering and frightened hands, so we begin to attain enlightenment when we—well, when we begin.

Before a man gains anything worth having he must want it, whether it is a job, a flat or salvation, and for anything of spiritual value he must want it, as the Zen Master said, as much as a man whose head is held under water wants air. For though unworthy desire must be eliminated, it is foolish to argue that all desire is evil, for if so with what do we strive to attain enlightenment? What, then, do we want? Pleasure? It is available. Happiness? Do we know what we mean by the term? And in the last analysis does it rise above material comfort and absence of responsibility? What do we count more worthy of our desire than these? Salvation? If so, of what, from what and by whom? It is important that these questions be answered, for of those who desire salvation few can answer them. The constant demand, though seldom admitted, is for some Power or Being or Force to save us from the well-earned consequences of our sins and with the minimum effort by the sinner. Yet there are those whose desire aims higher—for Enlightenment.

All great men worthy of the name have this in common, their tremendous size or scope of mind. A great man has a great mind, and the image springs to hand of space, of a sun-lit grandeur swept by the winds of heaven, and void, utterly void, of our human pettiness, or self. Enlightenment is a pregnant term, and so is awakening, one meaning of the root word *Budh* from which is derived the title *Buddha*, the Awakened One. Herein is no *avidya* left, no mist of uncertainty, no darkness of illusion. These are the marks of self-hood which lives in duality and difference; Enlightenment is the awareness of a Oneness beyond all difference, of a knowledge conscious and direct of the Absolute. Is this worth having, or even a foretaste of its unstained serenity?

Then what is the price that the would-be purchaser must pay, for nothing worth having may be had for the asking. There must be an immediate deposit of much time and thought and energy. Then dearer belongings must be sacrificed, in the religious sense, that is, made holy in the giving. All our prejudice must go, our dear opinions and entrenched beliefs, whether inherited or later acquired by solemn reasoning (and this is rare), or by chance formation from a first impression, or a neighbour's word. Our present sense of values must be forfeit, too, and a wiser set developed. For our likes and dislikes are seldom reasonable, and our place on this or the other side of the fence in politics or social life, as in most things wherein men have argument was seldom reasonably acquired. But however formed, these various conclusions—and the word means that which is shut up—will prove a hindrance to the cool, impersonal understanding which is a faculty of the great because enlightened mind.

In the end we must pay the final price, our most endeared possession, self. How shall a mind be great whose voice at all times cries, and cries but little else than, 'I . . . I . . . I'? Such is the payment, on the instalment system if you will, but yet continuous and painful in the extreme. Yet strangely enough, as payment is regularly made the purchaser becomes the greater and the richer for the deal. As self and its claims die out, as the dark and cluttered box-room of the mind is expanded into a mighty space wherein the sunlight and the mountain air sing happily, there will be no regrets for the convictions and beliefs which, now in the dustbin of the day's meditation, trouble the mind no more.

As the Buddhist pilgrim moves, and makes his sacrifice, his relationship to the Buddha-Dhamma will steadily progress. There are, perhaps, four phases on the Way. First, the static, 'I am interested in Buddhism'. Then, when the first step is taken: 'I use it', to be later reversed, at a moment vital to the pilgrim, and replaced with: 'Now the Buddha-Dhamma uses me'. Finally, the dawn of a joy which has no part with pleasure or happiness as usually conceived: 'I live for the Dhamma and in it, each moment of the day'. Only when the final stage is reached is Bodhicitta born in the heart, the living, enlightened awareness of the world as one. Then only, when each action is felt to be right because it is the action of the Whole, when the sense of duty and right and the joy of both is fused in a cool serenity, is born the experience of a Way on which no sense of haste, no thought of purpose or reward remains; where the opportunity of time is dissolved in a new-found sense of timing, and there is but the next thing to be joyously, impersonally done.

And who decides what is right, and what is one's duty? Who but you? There is no God to do it for you, no Authority to tell you what is true, or for that matter what is Buddhism. Study, and deeply, by all means, but as you move. Move and the Way will open, and the answers, all of them, appear.

But there are many obstructions on the Way, fallen tree-trunks, which, once beautiful, are now but a nuisance to all concerned. One is the God-concept which, though it serves its purpose for millions of Westerners, has no place in the Buddhist analysis of life. It may be an admirable conception, this Absolute yet personal Being who, in the intervals of creation of worlds and souls, finds time to assist each pilgrim in his personal affairs, but the Buddhist has no need of it. Yet the thought is not easily removed from a Western mind. Enlarge it, then. If the Absolute is inconceivable—'The Tao that can be expressed is not the eternal Tao'-substitute for the whim of a God the living Law of cause–effect, and assume the enormous dignity which grows from awareness that indeed we 'work out our own salvation with diligence'. Then will arise a sense of vast companionship with all that lives. Truly the heart is warmed to find that life is one, and that all its parts, the noblest and the least, are 'members one of another'.

A more serious obstacle in the Buddhist life is the network of illusions which enmesh the Western mind. One is the confusion of thought and emotion in valuing experience. The law of Karma, for example, is either true or untrue. If it be true it is irrelevant whether one likes it or not. The same applies to change, or selfless-ness, or the doctrine of rebirth. Yet a member of an audience will frequently announce, 'I do not like the idea of Karma. It sounds cold'. Or, 'I do not wish to come back to earth'. The reply is obvious, that we may not approve the law of gravity as we fall down a well, but the law still operates.

A more subtle error, held by minds great enough to know better, is to believe that the intellect can lead to Truth; whereas it only tells us more and more about it. The intellect deals with concepts, 'things' created by the mind of the substance of thought. Each is composed of a choice of the pairs of opposites, each of which is only partially true. However balanced the new confection of attributes, it is never Truth. The awareness of Truth, which lies in its very nature beyond reasoning, is achieved by the faculty of Buddhi, the intuition. This experience, though absolute for the experiencer, is unprovable, and indeed indescribable to another. The intellect, though a magnificent instrument, must be developed in order to transcend itself. Not until the light of Buddhi floods the field of thought is the dreary dichotomy of subject–object fused in the new awareness, the direct experience of Reality.

The third and last illusion is self. Only when self is analysed, and the student finds for himself that none of its parts is permanent, will this chattering monkey be quietened and in the end dissolved. Then the mind, in increasing harmony with All-Mind—and the nature of this is a matter of experience—knows itself as one with the universe, and an instrument in the evolution of the Whole. Wisdom–Compassion are found to be twin forces for the using, not for possession, and as room is made for them in place of self, the size and strength of these forces in the mind increase accordingly. Truly the great man is a power for good; he offers less and less resistance to the Light which, when it shines in any mind, is the light of Enlightenment.

With a lessening of illusion, and the growth of Mind in the mind, what a swift improvement is made in controlled reactions to the day's environment. Karma itself is found to be the most exciting of the new forces. Meditate but an hour on the fact that there is no luck, no chance, no fate and no coincidence in life. Then face the reverse. All things flow from a preceding cause; all things have an effect on all. One's lightest thought or emotion or deed has effect, on one plane or another, on all in the room, in the town, in the world, in the universe; and the littlest act of all in the country, on the earth, in the universe is affecting you. What new responsibility is here, and what complete removal of our favourite pastime, complaint? For why complain when you are to blame, you and your brothers-in-One?

The 'Signs of Being', when applied, can change our view of life profoundly. All must agree on the law of change, but how many live as though it were true? Is increasing age accepted or resisted; do we regard our possessions as held in trust for all, or as things which we have successfully attached to 'me', and the removal of which, from any cause, we deeply resent? There is no self, but we all fear death. Why, when it is inevitable from the moment of birth, and the only thing we do not know about it is the date? We agree that we move unceasingly to something different, yet we insure ourselves so that so far as possible nothing about ourselves shall change. We fear to lose our jobs or homes or children; seldom are we content to let slip our self-made moorings and to move unfettered, anchorless, upon the stream of experience down to the Shining Sea. As for suffering, who doubts that it pertains in all our being, in each moment of the day? Do we accept it as self-wrought, face it, digest it; in brief, experience it; or do we resent it and strive to escape, into pleasure, illusion, or death?

'Compassion is no attribute. It is the law of Laws, eternal harmony . . . a shoreless universal essence, the light of everlasting right, and fitness of all things, the Law of Love eternal.' Such is the Law—do we live by it? He is a most unusual man who habitually looks on his fellow men as brothers, as pilgrims on the same path to the same distant Goal, and behaves to them accordingly. Yet if life *is* one, and the least form of it holy with that life, why is a world that should be learning by the experience ever at war? Because each man is at war within, and not until the war is won for compassion against the powers of hatred, lust and illusion of separation in each individual mind will the mass-mind of a nation, or of the few who direct it, truly want what only then they will achieve, peace.

The sweetly reasonable Four Noble Truths are clearly true, that we suffer, and that the cause of our suffering is self. Do we, from dawn to bedtime, strive to remove that cause? Yet the mere analysis of the thing called 'I' will soon work wonders. When temper is lost, who lost control of what? What fears that this and this will happen, and does it matter if it does? These fearsome happenings we fear, if we let them come shall we wake in the morning? We shall! These problems that we fear to face, who made them? We made them, with a combination of reasoning, usually bad reasoning, and emotion, in itself a cause of suffering. Let us walk up to the problem, in full awareness that it does not exist outside our mind. It will not be easy to reach it, for as we approach it moves away, like the morning mist on the road that looks so solid ahead but which, as we move towards it, is never reached. We made the problem and threw it ahead upon the Way. We approach and are frightened by it. Yet if we still walk on it is never there. As Dr Graham Howe said of the precipice ahead of us, 'Some stop at the sight of it; some go round, or try to. Some go back. Why not go on and over?' This is at least most admirable Zen.

How, then, do we travel up the mountain side, in the acquisition and digestion of direct experience? Is the chosen path the gradual or the sudden ascent; the gentle spiral, with seats at chosen intervals from which to admire the view, or the fierce, direct, unpausing 'sudden' way of Zen? Choose as you will, for neither is right or wrong, nor better, and a long way up the hill they are seen to converge at a point which need not trouble us until we reach it. Both paths begin in the worldly life, with what is to hand, and here, and now. Both need the co-ordination of mind and will and all that we have of mental and moral 'guts' to enable us to keep going. Both are a Middle

Way between all extremes, in the course of which the inward tension of the mind is slowly raised for the ultimate assault upon illusion, the slaying of the dragon of self, the awakening, when the final veil is torn away, to the light of Enlightenment.

Each way is an approach to the Absolute; in each the effort is perpetual, and is made in the worldly life until right effort has enabled the climber to train for the final assault on Reality. The Theravada is the more solemn way, with something of the Puritan ideal. The Zen way is more joyous, and carefree; and indeed, being frankly irrational, it is free of the concepts, precepts, rules and milestones of the Arhat's introspective concentration. 'Let the mind abide no-where, and alight upon nothing', says the Diamond Sutra. And how shall it not when all is indeed an interdiffusion of *sunyata*, Void of all things whatever?

'Move and the Way will open'. This is the heart of Buddhism for it is the first and last word on the Way. The greatest scriptures of the world alike proclaim right action. The *Bhagavad Gita* is indeed a manual of right action, of the correct tactics in the war within; the *Dhammapada* is a moral-philosophy of action equally applicable without and within. The *Tao Te Ching* is by its very title the Way of Tao, of the virtue of Tao in action. 'When one looks at it, one cannot see it. When one listens to it, one cannot hear it. But when one uses it, it is inexhaustible'. Christ spoke of the mystical unity of the Way. 'I am the Way, the Truth and the Life'; and *The Voice of the Silence,* perhaps the oldest Scripture of them all, makes it clearer still. 'Thou canst not travel on the Path before thou hast become that Path itself'.

Let us arise then, and not only seek experience, direct, immediate experience, but be unafraid when we find it. How? The answer is another question: 'Who holds you back?' Let it be said again, for there is no more to be said. There are two rules upon the Way—Begin and Continue. Asked, 'What is Tao?', a master replied, 'Walk on'.

19

Should Buddhists Meditate?

Buddhism is the largest field of human thought, and the history of Buddhism shows that when the Teaching reached a new country the inhabitants of that country would choose, of this wide range of philosophy, morality, metaphysics, religion, ritual and culture, those aspects or doctrines most helpful to their spiritual needs. Thus the Buddhism of Tibet, of China and of Japan is in outward form and relative emphasis widely different from the Theravada, and each is different from each other.

The same has applied in the West, meaning, largely, the Nordic or Anglo-Saxon element in Europe and the USA. In England 50 years ago the emphasis among the handful of Buddhists was on Karma and Rebirth and the Eightfold Middle Way. Other doctrines have risen to priority as generations succeeded one another, and for some years past the 'fashionable' element in Buddhism, assisted by the equivalent in Yoga, has been meditation, even though many who practise 'meditation' do not know what they are doing or why. These practitioners look to the East for guidance, taking it according to the teacher's country of origin, whether Sri Lanka, Thailand, Tibet or Japan.

How essential is meditation for the Western Buddhist? Clearly it will be confined to the few dedicated Buddhists, for whom the Dhamma is central. After all, the majority of people in a Buddhist country merely pay lip-service to the Founder, practise occasional ritual or some form of devotion at a shrine on a festival occasion, and bear in mind a general regard for the

Buddhist way of life. The same applies in England, where only a small percentage of the thousands interested actually dedicate their lives to the practice of the Dhamma.

What, by way of meditation, do these few people do? What should they do, and how and when and above all why? To these questions there can be no dogmatic answer. Each must work out his own salvation with diligence, and be allowed the liberty to do so. If called upon to help, one must take into account the stage achieved by the enquirer on the Way. Is he a 'beginner', coming to Buddhism for the first time? Or clearly a developed mind which, failing to find elsewhere the Way desired turns to that offered by the All-Enlightened One? Or is this seeker near the Goal?

Again, one must allow for types of mind or character. The Hindus speak of the Juana Yogin, the man of Wisdom versed in the Doctrine, with deep understanding of the Buddha-mind; of the Bhakti Yogin, who follows the way of devotion to some beloved Ideal, enshrined, it may be, in some beloved Guru; and of the Karma Yogin, the man of action, of 'right' action, as portrayed in the *Bhagavad Gita*. And we in the West have Carl Jung's famous analysis of human types into the introvert and extravert, whose attitude to life is fundamentally different but complementary. When the permutations of these types and their stage of growth is analysed, it becomes impossible to answer easily what meditation means to each.

In the West, two radically different views are held. At one extreme is the teacher who considers that Buddhism and meditation are co-terminous, that the first duty of anyone coming into Buddhism is to sit down and meditate, so that he may learn something of himself before he takes any further step. At the other extreme are those, and not so uncommon, who hold that meditation in any form is quite unsuited to the Western mind, and that the practice is no more needed than the presence of the Sangha in our midst. Others again take a middle way between these two extremes. First, they suggest, let the would-be Buddhist learn to concentrate his mind on a chosen object or theme, at will, for a considerable time. Until the mind is a tool to be used at will, a servant taught to obey, a faculty under considerable control, it is useless to talk of meditation. And such practice is in no way religious, much less spiritual, but a stage which cannot be bypassed. Then let current ideas be examined, and most of them discarded, such as belief in a Saviour. Only then, in a mind cleansed of some of its illusion, will there be room for new, in the sense of strange and different, doctrines to be studied, digested, applied until they begin to grow roots and flower in new awareness. Such deep study and thought will in time merge in true meditation, whether the physical position used be something from the East or, more comfortable, upright on a chair.

In London, there is much discussion on this question of priorities. I know of no passage in the Pali Canon where the Buddha says to a new arrival, having no previous knowledge of the religious life in any form, 'Sit, and meditate'. Rather, the relative importance of well-known aspects of the religious life are clearly set out, in the famous trilogy of *dana, sila, bhavana,* where bhavana, the 'making-to-become' by mind control, is subsequent to or at least coterminous with dana, giving, and true morality. Again, in the *Dhammapada* we read, 'Cease to do evil; learn to do good; cleanse your own heart. This is the religion of the Buddhas'. The cleansing of the heart, in meditation practices, comes only when the whole life has become, at least to some extent, dedicated to the service of all, and at least harmless to one's fellow men.

I believe this order to be of profound importance, and it brings me to the question which every would-be Buddhist should be asked, demanding a true, full answer, WHY? Why does this person wish to learn to meditate? I know from long experience what is the reason in many of those who strive to learn. It is threefold, in lessening degrees of utter wrongness. First, to develop 'powers', meaning in fact the lower psychic faculties, possession of which will serve to inflate the person's ego, increase his selfishness, lead to the abuse of the powers so gained and bind him further on the Wheel. Next, to escape, from a temporary situation, from the long, hard road of life among men, or even from life itself into a world of phantasy. And, finally, a genuine mistake, in the belief that the will can force upon the mind a 'peace of mind' which any Eastern guru, Zen master or other teacher with spiritual experience, and any trained psychiatrist in the West, will agree to be quite impossible. For the manifested universe is built upon the pairs of opposites, is in perpetual tension between them, and will be so until that individual mind has passed beyond both, has reached the 'other shore' of Nirvana, has freed himself from the Wheel, or, in the words of Zen Buddhism, has broken through from duality to Non-duality. Till then the mind is ceaselessly at war; we are indeed warriors in this sense, as the Buddha proclaimed.

Motive, or rather, right motive will alone put meditation in its proper place in the dedicated life, and keep it there. And when right motive, the service of mankind, deliberate dedication to the needs of all that is born of the Unborn, is clearly and finally dominant, there will be time enough to look to the specific purpose, something very different from motive, of meditation of any kind. I know of four main purposes, and the practice used must be chosen accordingly.

First, to rouse, or raise, to become one with the Unconscious. This must be a long process, and sooner or later, when the student is truly ready, involve long hours of meditation at a time. There have been schools of such in the Christian fold from the very beginning, and in religious Orders of various names since time immemorial. The koan technique of Zen Buddhism is a case in hand. Second, to improve the quality of the mind, or raise the level of habitual consciousness. To build in qualities desired and to let die the opposite. An example would be the Brahma Viharas or phrases from the *Dhammapada*, such as 'Hatred ceaseth not by hatred, hatred ceaseth but by love'. But here again the practitioner must beware of the reaction from the unconscious. Third, for the devotional type, full concentration on and surrender to, the will of the Beloved. In the field of Buddhism there is much of this type in Tibet, and in Japan, for example in Shin Buddhism. And finally, to assist the day's 'right action', each act carried out with right motive, right means, at the right time and place and quite impersonally, because it is the next thing to be done.

These have, of course, a great deal in common. In all of them the oldest and surely the best beginning is the breathing exercise known in the Pali Canon as *anapanasati*, watching the breaths as a specific aid to being permanently 'mindful and self-possessed'. This is itself an exercise in the destruction of the ego. For the air which flows in and out is not yours or mine. This 'I' is but a temporary, ever-changing manifestation of the Unborn. There is no separate 'self' save in our false imagining. But 'belly-watching', as a famous Bhikkhu in Ceylon described it, is foolish, first because by producing a 'closed circuit' of force onto this part of the 'self' it strengthens concentration on 'my belly'; second, because it tends to rouse the lower psychic powers by wakening the forces of the chakra to be found nearby; and third, as that learned doctor-bhikkhu seemed to be aware, it can have grave physiological results.

But when the beginner has learned to concentrate, when his motive and purpose are at least clearer to him than they were, and when he feels the need, let him begin to meditate, as and where and when he will. But not until. We had a severe lesson in this in England, when a group of enquirers was becoming well established in a town in the provinces until they invited a bhikkhu to talk to them. He told them to meditate and talked of nothing else. Six months later the group had melted away. They did not *want* to meditate. They wanted to learn about Buddhism!

When should one meditate? Clearly a regular time each day is all but the best advice. The best, I believe, is to encourage the would-be Buddhist to cultivate, however slowly, a new permanent state of mind, a dedicated use of the whole day, of work and rest, of joy and sorrow, triumph and despair, to the

Dhamma and the Way to the heart's release from suffering. One of the Founders of the Theosophical Society called it 'wearing the Yellow Robe internally'. Only those who have to some extent succeeded in this quest know the result of it. New energy and the deep content of dedication; new vision of the plan and purpose of the manifested universe, of the Life-energy we perceive in a million forms; new conscious contact with the Beyond of Samsara, the state which Buddhists call Nirvana, or the 'Unborn, Unoriginated, Unformed', or just the Beyond. In this pursuit we can be busy all the day, helping all men to the same content of mind. This and no less can be the fruit of meditation practised happily, unceasingly, for the one right motive and right purpose, the salvation of all mankind.

Concentration and Meditation

'Meditation', says Dr Evans-Wentz in his Foreword to Miss Lounsbery's *Buddhist Meditation,* 'is the royal highway to man's understanding of himself'. This magnificent statement is profoundly true. In the words of a Buddhist Scripture, 'Cease to do evil; learn to do good; cleanse your own heart. This is the Teaching of the Buddhas'. First comes the dual process of abandoning wrong ways of thought and action and developing those which reflect the One and are therefore 'right'. But then there opens the true and final Path, the assault on illusion, the illusion of self and all its works, for the life of morality is only a preparation for the ultimate reunion of mind with Mind. The Buddhist Goal is the full Enlightenment of the individual mind, a process wherein the light flows in as the man-made barriers of self are slowly cleared away. This process, as often pointed out, is not the salvation of a soul but the liberation of the Self from self, of the individual mind from the illusion of separation. The process of self-liberation is therefore confined to the individual mind, though carried out for the ultimate benefit of all. It follows that no task is more important to the Buddhist; all else, the acquiring of knowledge, moral improvement, and even the practice of 'right' action are secondary, and in themselves of no complete avail. The reason is obvious, for in Buddhist teaching, 'All that we are is the result of what we have thought; it is founded on our thoughts, it is made up of our thoughts'. In the cyclic process of becoming mind is paramount, for it is the thoughts begotten in the mind which manifest as action, 'good' or 'bad', according as the act moves towards Oneness or away from it; when the thought is right, right action follows.

The Buddhist Way, then, is a process of self-liberation of the individual mind, and the planned and unceasing work of mental purification and expansion fills the working day. The methods used have varied with the schools of thought developed in the vast field of Buddhism. In the West, the technique of the Theravada is best known, and it may be useful to give here an outline of its technique. The argument runs: All men are suffering, and suffering from the fires of lust, hatred and illusion. The fault is theirs, and arises from the illusion of self. As this illusion resides in the mind, the mind must be purified by a strenuous course of training which will destroy the illusion, and produce instead the conscious awareness of Reality in which there is Mind-Only and no self. This *Bhavana*, or process of mental liberation, has two stages. The first is *Satipatthana*, in which the mind is controlled, trained to see things as they are without emotion or thought of self, and prepared as a hand-wrought instrument for the final approach to Enlightenment. The second stage is to transcend the limitations of the instrument thus made. But only by mind can the mind be transcended, and there is no short-cut which avoids the early stages of the process; only through a controlled and well-developed mind can the final stage of No-Mind, which is All-Mind, be achieved. The spiritual insight or *Vipassanā* so gained equates with the Satori of Zen, but the true relation between these and other exalted states of consciousness is a matter too advanced, and too debatable, to be considered here.

In the course of *Satipatthana* the four *Jhanas*, advanced stages of consciousness, are reached and transcended, and various *Iddhis*, supernormal powers, are incidentally developed. All this is well set out in *The Heart of Buddhist Meditation*, by the Ven. Nyanaponika Thera, but a teacher is essential for this strenuous course of training, and the student wishing to use it should apply for the assistance which he needs.

In the West, the need for some guidance in mind-development was made acute some 35 years ago by a sudden spate of books which were, whatever the motive of their authors, dangerous in the extreme. No word was said in them of the sole right motive for mind-development, the enlightenment of the meditator for the benefit of all mankind, and the reader was led to believe that it was quite legitimate to study and practise mindfulness, and the higher stages which ensue, for the benefit of business efficiency and the advancement of personal prestige. In these circumstances *Concentration and Meditation,* a hand-book written for the Western mind, was many years ago compiled and published by the Buddhist Society, with constant stress on the importance of right motive, and ample warning of the dangers, from a headache to insanity, which lie in wait for those who trifle with the greatest force on earth, the human mind. At the same time Miss Lounsbery, of Les Amis du Bouddhisme in Paris, published her *Buddhist Meditation in the Southern School,* stressing the same advice to beginners as given in our own more catholic work. Both books emphasize the need of practice, as distinct from theory; for as Dr Evans-Wentz pointed out in his Introduction to Miss Lounsbery's book, 'Buddhism emphasizes that the realization of Truth is incomparably more important than belief in Truth; that religious faith and devotion, being merely the first steps on the Path, are themselves not enough; that if Truth is to be realized, there must be Right Belief, Right Intentions, Right Speech, Right Actions, Right Means of Livelihood, Right Endeavouring, Right Mindfulness, Right Meditation'. In other words, to use an old analogy, it is useless to sit in an armchair at a point whence a dozen roads lead off in various directions, and merely to consider the merits of each and the nature of the goal at the end of them. It is better to rise and tread the first steps along one of them than to consider the whole of them and to practise none. Indeed, so important is the need for practice in meditation that it has been said there are two rules for a new practitioner, 'Begin, and Continue'! In the practice of both rules the quality of *tamas*, inertia, will strenuously resist the will. If it is hard to plan and begin the long period of effort, it is far more difficult to continue, and only the early results, greater control of thought, serenity of mind and inner quietude persuade the beginner that the effects are worth the effort to produce them.

One of the earliest difficulties is the choice of English terms. *Samma Sati*, the seventh step on the Eightfold Path, is well translated as Right Mindfulness, but the eighth, *Samma* (or full) *Samadhi*, is often given as Right Concentration. In truth the term is untranslatable, but the three words used in *Concentration and Meditation* to describe the entire process are perhaps the most helpful and will here be used. Concentration is the creation of the instrument; meditation is the right use of it; contemplation transcends it. In the early stages, the first two should be kept separate, for different considerations apply; finally, all are merged in the One-Mind.

Concentration, which is a term far wider than 'attentiveness', an early stage of *Satipatthana*, certainly begins with the practice of attention, full, impersonal, objective attention to the task or thing in hand. All successful business men acquire this faculty, for without it the day's work is impossible. It is in no way 'spiritual', being only the power of sustained and directed thought. It is harder to turn the same faculty within. A man who is proud of his ability to concentrate in the presence of distraction will be quite unable to turn the searchlight of his thought on to the nature and process of his thinking. The West is extravert, its power turned on the nature and use of external forces, whether of money, politics or the Niagara Falls. The older East is essentially introvert, its values being sought within, and the criterion of value being the mind's expansion in understanding as distinct from the worldly power of the personality. In either event the mind must be broken to harness and yoked to its owner's will, an immensely difficult task, as all who strive to focus thought on a chosen subject find. 'As a fletcher straightens his arrows, so the wise man straightens his unsteady mind, which is hard indeed to control.' From the choice of a subject which arises in the course of 'normal life', such as doing accounts, drafting an agreement or a complex piece of knitting, to a choice made for the sake of an exercise in self-control is a large step, and the mind jibs at it. At first the subject may be external, a rose, a distant view, or the door-knob; then a subjective object, i.e. a subject, will be taken. Breathing itself may be used, or the body as such, the emotions in their permutations, or the incredibly swift rise and fall of thoughts within the mind. Miss Lounsbery points out that interest helps the power to concentrate; it is only at a later stage that the power is developed to concentrate by an effort of will on something without interest or, and this is of more value, to find interest in that which is, in all the circumstances, the next thing to be done.

Only when the mind is trained to obedience, as a small dog may be trained to come to heel when called (and to stay there), is the student in a fit state to begin to meditate. Immediately new rules apply; new aspects of the laws of life begin to operate. The would-be saviour of himself and all mankind is moving ahead of his fellow men. He is developing powers not known to, much less possessed by those of his own intellectual standing. Just as magic is a knowledge of the laws of nature not yet possessed by scientists, much less by the common herd, so meditation quickly develops powers not yet possessed by the most efficient business man. Why, then, the teacher may ask the pupil, do you meditate, giving your time and thought and energy to mental development not yet achieved by most of your fellow men? It is vital that the answer be true and clear. There is one sole motive for self-advancement which is right, and it is not the aggrandisement of self. Indeed, as the inner development continues, the personality grows less, and with the withdrawal of energy from its worldly affairs it may tend to fade out in the eyes of men. The sole motive for meditation is to purge the self of illusion, to develop the faculty of intuition to the point of Enlightenment, and to desire this Enlightenment, if desired at all, for the sake of the One-Mind. Anything less is evil, an abuse of powers, and the karma of such misuse is terrible. Think well, then, before you begin to meditate, and see that the reason for your vast new effort is right.

For the first time physical habits become important. There are ample reasons for the right posture to be observed, for the time to be regular, and the place, if possible, the same. To strain is foolish, for the process must be slow, but if the practice is well conceived and regular, results will appear. Some of them will be unwelcome, and psychic visions and noises, emotional disturbances and alarming dreams may deter the would-be Arhat. The mental hindrances are worse. Miss Lounsbery mentions five; craving, ill will, sloth, agitated states of mind and doubt. I have myself found many more. But the rewards are commensurate. There is quietude of body, as of emotions, and the dying down of the fires of lust and hatred which burn so tediously within the mind. Thought is steadied, strengthened and increasingly brought under control. The newly acquired impersonality of thinking, with thoughts bereft of emotion and the constant reference to 'I', brings the clear light of a new serenity, and love acquires new meaning. It is compassion now which speaks, with the voice of the Silence, and provides the 'right' because un-selfish motive for every act.

This new affection for all fellow forms of life can be canalized in useful action. The four *Brahma Viharas*, for example, can be usefully exercised at any time and place, from the office to a restaurant, from a dentist's waiting-room to a bus. These four virtues, though powers of the mind is a better term, are Metta, loving-kindness or good-will, Karuna, compassion, Mudita, sympathetic joy and Upekkha, equanimity of mind. In a famous quotation from a Buddhist Sutta, 'He lets his mind pervade one quarter of the world with thoughts of *metta,* with thoughts of *karuna,* with thoughts of *mudita* and with thoughts of *upekkha;* and so for the second quarter, and so the third and so the fourth. And thus the whole wide world above, below, around and everywhere does he continue to pervade with heart of love, compassion, joy and equanimity, far-reaching, great, beyond measure, free from the least trace of anger or ill-will'.

The subjects of meditation are all but infinite. All virtues may be used, and noble thoughts, for as Epictetus, the Greek slave, said, 'You must know that it is no easy thing for a principle to become a man's own, unless each day he maintain it and hear it maintained, as well as work it out in life'. And how shall it be better maintained and applied than in constantly meditating upon it? Any phrase will do from a thinker or poet who speaks the eternal Wisdom, and in *Concentration and Meditation* a few score suggestions are made. Some in the West object to a few of the practices of *Satipatthana,* such, for example, as the meditations on a corpse or in a graveyard, designed to bring home the truth of *anicca,* change. Certainly, these are not suitable to the beginner, and are only mentioned here to remove the belief that Eastern meditation largely consists in such practices. They are in fact but a brief stage in the slow and complete withdrawal of the mind from sense attachment, and have their uses, as some of us even of the West well know.

But it is always easier to keep up the pressure in a long and graded task like mind-development if there is a definite course prescribed. There are many such in Buddhism, and the student should decide his own. Thereafter what matters is persistence, and the due effects will follow the unremitting pressure of the cause. The whole range of *Satipatthana,* right mindfulness, is available to London students with competent instructors, but this, as all other systems of the Theravada, limits its ideals to the Arhat, the self-perfected individual who works for his own liberation in the belief that until he has purged his own mind from the snares of self he cannot usefully assist mankind. To a man or woman of the complementary temperament this cold, impersonal analysis, and subsequent training of the mind to the smooth efficiency of a beautiful machine, is insufficient to supply their total needs. The Mahayana range is wide and equally available, the hardest to practise being the joyous, inconsequent and almost non-sensical technique of Zen, which aims at no less than sudden and immediate, direct Enlightenment, in flashes at first but later as a fully developed faculty of the mind. It would seem, though the point is debatable, that Zen technique should begin when the mind has already reached a fairly advanced stage of right mindfulness. Not until the intellect is well developed and controlled can it be transcended; yet until it is transcended the Absolute of the One Mind can never be truly known. To the extent that Zen has a specified ideal it shares the Bodhisattva doctrine of the Mahayana schools, but the man who is dedicated to the service of all Life, and in particular to his fellow human beings, must still perfect himself if he wishes to be of better service than a vague goodwill, and the Arhat and the Bodhisattva ideals are complementary as the two sides of a coin.

From Concentration to Meditation, from Meditation to Contemplation, such are the stages, and of the third stage little can usefully be said. At this level of consciousness, whether known as *Vipassana, Satori, Samadhi,* or by any other name, all words are slightly ridiculous. As is said in the *Lankavatara Sutra,* 'If you assert that there is such a thing as Noble Wisdom it no longer holds good, for anything of which something is asserted thereby partakes of the nature of being, and thus has the quality of birth. The very assertion, 'All things are un-born, destroys the truthfulness of it'. For it is clear to the intellect that every statement is short of truth, for its opposite must, in the Absolute, be equally true. All pairs of opposites are relative, and only of value and meaning in a relative world. 'The Tao that can be expressed is not the eternal Tao', and descriptions of Nirvana, or the same experience by another name, are demonstrably untrue.

Contemplation, as I defined it in opening this section in the book entitled *Concentration and Meditation,* 'is an utterly impersonal awareness of the essence of the thing observed'. When self is purged from the mind of the observer, the trinity of seer, seen and the seeing is dissolved, and the seer sees by becoming the essence of the thing observed. The operative word is essence, as distinct from the inessential form. For the essence of all things alike is *tathata,* the suchness of things, and this suchness is Void (*sunya*), of all particulars. Only a mind in the void is No-Mind, resting in the state of no-thinking or Mu-shin, and only the mind that has reached such a stage for a second or an hour can speak—and he cannot speak of it—of the utter serenity and power that flows from Life itself into a mind that sets no barrier against its flow. But these are the fruits of *Bhavana,* using the term for meditation in its widest sense. The tree must grow from an acorn to an oak before the fruit appears. First come the exercises backed by right motive and an indomitable will; then the right use of the new-won instrument. Only then comes the nakedness of a mind new cleansed of its own self-wrought illusion. This is freedom indeed, yet—asked by a pupil, 'Master, how shall I free my mind?' the Master replied, 'Who puts you under restraint?'

Empty the Mind

Empty the mind and let the teeming void
In silence speak. Be still and let the dearth
Of sound and sight be fruitfully employed.
Empty the mind of all that men of earth,
With choice and valuation, fretful thought,
Self-laden aspiration, use to fill
The corridors of being and with wrought
Impediment frustrate the teeming will.
Empty the mind, and life, pure life, shall flow
Unsullied with the day's duality
Till utterly the true heart-mind shall know,
Nor fear, the void of full totality.

Glossary

Sk — Sanskrit, P — Pali, Chin — Chinese, Jap — Japanese

ANATTA (P). The essentially Buddhist doctrine of non-ego.

ANICCA (P). Impermanence. One of the three characteristics of existence: the others being *Dukkha* and *Anatta*.

ARHAT. A Worthy one. The ideal of the Theravada School.

ATMAN (Sk). The Supreme Self; Universal Consciousness.

AVIDYA (Sk). Ignorance; lack of enlightenment.

BHAKTI (Sk). Devotion to a spiritual ideal.

BHAVANA (Sk & P). Self-development by any means, but especially by the method of mind-control, concentration and meditation.

BODHISATTVA (Sk). One whose 'being' or 'essence' (*sattva*) is *Bodhi*. The wisdom resulting from direct perception of Truth, with the compassion awakened thereby.

BRAHMAN (Sk). The impersonal and supreme Principle of the Universe.

BUDDHA. A title meaning Awakened, in the sense of enlightened. The founder of Buddhism in the sixth century BC.

BUDDHI (Sk). The vehicle of enlightenment (Bodhi). The faculty of direct awareness of Reality. The intuition.

DANA (Sk & P). Giving. Benevolence.

DHARMA (Sk), DHAMMA (P). System, doctrine, law, truth, cosmic order (according to the context). The Buddhist teaching.

DHYANA (Sk). Meditation. A stage on the way to Prajna (q.v.). The Japanese derivation of the word is Zen which, however, has a very different meaning.

DUKKHA (P). Suffering, in any form and from any cause.

JHANA (P). State of serene contemplation attained by meditation.

KAMA (Sk). Desire of the senses, especially sexual desire. The craving arising from the false belief in an ego or self separate from the rest of manifestation.

KARMA (Sk). The law of cause and effect, as applied to the mind. It is not limited by time and space, and is not strictly individual. The doctrine of Rebirth is an essential corollary to that of Karma.

KARUNA (Sk). Active compassion, cf. prajna.

KOAN (Jap). A word or phrase creating a problem that cannot be solved by reasoning or thought. An exercise for breaking the limitation of thought and developing the intuition.

186

MAHAYANA. The Buddhist School of the Great Vehicle (of liberation); also called the Northern School (Tibet, Mongolia, China, Korea and Japan).

MANAS (Sk). Mind. The rational faculty in man.

MAYA (Sk). Illusion, popularly used in this sense. Philosophically, the phenomenal universe, being subject to differentiation and impermanence is Maya.

MONDO (Jap). Questions and Answers. The short, pithy dialogues between Zen masters and their disciples.

NIRVANA (Sk). The supreme goal of Buddhist endeavour; release from the limitations of separate existence. A state attainable in this life. One who has attained to this state is called *arhat*.

PALI. One of the early languages of Buddhism, later adopted by the Theravadins as the language in which to preserve the memorised teachings of the Buddha.

PARAMITA (Sk). Perfection. The six (or ten) stages of spiritual perfection followed by the Bodhisattva in his progress to Buddhahood.

PRAJNA (Sk). Transcendental wisdom. One of the paramitas.

RAGA (P). Greed; passion; uncontrolled lust of any kind.

SAMADHI. Contemplation on reality. The eighth step on the Eightfold path.

SAMSARA (Sk & P). Continued 'coming-to-be'. Existence in the world as compared with Nirvana.

SAMSKARA (Sk), SANKHARA (P). One of the five *skandhas* (q.v.). Contents of the mind at any one moment which will condition the functioning of consciousness and, in turn, be influenced by that functioning.

SATORI (Jap). A term of Zen Buddhism. State of consciousness beyond the plane of discrimination and differentiation.

SILA (Sk & P). The Buddhist code of morality.

SKANDHA (Sk). The five causally-conditioned elements of existence forming a (temporary) being or entity. They are inherent in every form of life, either in active or potential state.

SUNYATA (Sk). Voidness. Doctrine asserting the voidness of ultimate reality. Abolishes all concepts of dualism and proclaims the essential oneness of the phenomenal and noumenal.

TAO (Chin). The central concept of Taoism, as expressed in the *Tao Te Ching*. Can mean the One and the Way to it.

THERAVADA (P). The 'Doctrine of the Elders' who formed the first Buddhist Council. The School of Buddhism of Ceylon, Burma and Thailand.

VIJNANA (Sk). Consciousness; the faculty by which one cognizes the phenomenal world.

VIPASSANA (P). Insight; Intuitive vision. Also a system of meditation practised in Theravada—'right mindfulness'.

ZEN (Jap). A corruption of the Chinese *Ch'an* which in turn is derived from the Sanskrit Dhyana. The School of Zen Buddhism which passed from China to Japan in the thirteenth and fourteenth centuries.

Index